August '93

To Lola,

from your friend

& your friends Martinez y
Judy — Love,

Love Match

LOVE
MATCH

Nelson vs. Navratilova

BY
Sandra Faulkner
WITH
Judy Nelson

INTRODUCTION BY
Rita Mae Brown

A Birch Lane Press Book
Published by Carol Publishing Group

The opinions of the authors of *Love Match* are their own, and not those of other individuals referred to throughout the work.

A Birch Lane Press Book
Published by Carol Publishing Group
Birch Lane Press is a registered trademark of Carol Communications, Inc.
Editorial Offices: 600 Madison Avenue, New York, N.Y. 10022
Sales and Distribution Offices: 120 Enterprise Avenue, Secaucus, N.J. 07094
In Canada: Canadian Manda Group, P.O. Box 920, Station U, Toronto, Ontario M8Z 5P9
Queries regarding rights and permissions should be addressed to Carol Publishing Group, 600 Madison Avenue, New York, N.Y. 10022

Carol Publishing Group books are available at special discounts for bulk purchases, for sales promotion, fund-raising, or educational purposes. Special editions can be created to specifications. For details, contact: Special Sales Department, Carol Publishing Group, 120 Enterprise Avenue, Secaucus, N.J. 07094

Manufactured in the United States of America

10 9 8 7 6 5 4 3 2 1

Library of Congress Cataloging-in-Publication Data

Faulkner, Sandra.
 Love match : Nelson vs. Navratilova / by Sandra Faulkner with Judy Nelson.
   p.   cm.
 ISBN 1-55972-157-X
 1. Navratilova, Martina, 1956-   . 2. Nelson, Judy. 3. Lesbian couples—United States—Biography.   4. Tennis players—United States—Biography.   I. Nelson, Judy.   II. Title.
HQ75.3.F38   1993
796.342'092—dc20
[B]   92-39828
                                                   CIP

For my mother, Virginia, in grateful acknowledgment of the unconditional love she has given to each of her children.

Sandra Faulkner

To my sons, my parents, and my brother and sister, who have stood by me and given me unconditional love. To the gay friends who have embraced me and the straight friends who have not forsaken or judged me. And to Rita Mae Brown, whose wit has made me laugh again, and whose intelligence has always inspired me.

Judy Nelson

Contents

I am forever grateful to Rita Mae, Annie, Debbie, Jane and Trish, Mindy, Julie and Gigi, Clare, Chris, Chantal, Michael, Sandra, Jaye, BeAnn, Jerry, Marilyn, Beth, Philippe, Charles, Jim, Jane, Mimi, Bunny and Missy, Jane and Linda, and M.A. and her family. You were my strength when I had none. You were my light when everything was dark. You made me laugh when I had only tears. Because of you, with you, and through you, I found myself. You are each in my heart forever, and I love you all.

Judy Nelson

Introduction

Divorce may be the only human disaster that translates into money as well as giggles: money for the two involved and giggles for the rest of us as the adversaries rise to the heights of postamorous recrimination. The survivors of these battles are hors de combat—or is it whores de combat? Whatever, no one is ever quite the same after divorce.

When the fruits of collusion once ripe turn sour and are played out on the great pulpit of television, it's a major spectacle. When the two rivals are women, it is scandal too good to be true. Those who peddle uplift and relish downfall ascend to hog heaven. There was a lot of oinking over the Nelson-Navratilova split.

What a jolly amount of squealing from those who pronounced that lesbianism is not part of women's tennis, only part of Martina's life. Then there was the grunting of the hogs at the trough, frightened that the lovers' separation might temporarily reduce the amount of slops. At least the hogs in Washington are more practiced in covering up their greed. Finally, the sports media and entertainment media took upon themselves the laborious burden of presenting this split to the public. The ratings, of course, were secondary to this unselfish public service.

Modesty forbids that I mention the lawyers—just in case children should pick up this book.

During this trial-by-publicity two women whom I love dearly struggled to keep going, to refrain from the blasts of rage they sometimes felt, and to try and find some good in the day. I've been aware of Martina since she was fifteen years old. I've known her well since she was twenty. I've known Judy for eight years. Obviously, as I have been closer to Martina, you would expect me to take her side. In many ways, I have, but I can also see Judy's story, too, so perhaps it wasn't such a strange idea to ask me to write an introduction to Judy Nelson's book.

At first glance, one is hard put to find two women more different than Martina Navratilova and Judy Nelson. The former, a professional athlete raised in a then Communist country, lives the life of a tennis gypsy. It's a world in which velocity is confused with achievement. Fortunately, Martina was able to be successful in this peripatetic existence, finding a stability denied many on the road.

Judy Nelson was the quintessential American girl, a latter-day Doris Day singing as she ironed shirts for her man. Beautiful in the conventional sense and well rewarded for it, Judy speaks in a carefully cultivated feminine voice and has a clothes closet that rivals Imelda Marcos's. She married and produced an heir and a spare, a requirement of certain social class. If Martina's nine Wimbledon singles titles are her fulfillment then Judy's two sons are hers. Both women are justifiably proud.

But you can see how opposite they are. How they ever got together and stayed together for nearly eight years is a miracle. As for their split, that's less a miracle, but is there ever an easy way to say goodbye? If there is, Martina hasn't found it. She belongs to the Mario Andretti school of departure: put the pedal to the metal and get the hell out of Dodge.

Conventional morality demands that people cluck their tongues and shake their forefingers at that naughty Martina. This gasoline-soaked method may not be the most emotionally mature way of making an exit, but is it really any better to continue a defunct relationship ad infinitum? My observations of this method is that each party turns into a ruthless monologist chanting her tales of discontent into a litany of romantic victimization. Have you ever heard a man or woman say, "I was wrong"? Hardly. The less skilled at this procedure just list the sins of the other party now perceived as "the enemy." The better educated or more sly will generally assume some responsibility for the demise of the relationship while describing the formerly beloved as a passive-aggressive, or you-name-it. Martina spares us that.

Leaving Judy was a cycle of renewal for Martina. She had every right to go. The sticking point is whether she—or anyone—owes anything to the former partner. If both parties enjoy well-defined careers the answer is probably very little. However, if one party supports the other—a wife in convention-al terms—that creates untold difficulties.

Martina hasn't been trained to feel responsible for a partner once the bloom is off the rose. As far as I know, no woman has ever been inculcated into this way of thinking toward another woman. For her not to accept this or to grasp the concept seems no great sin to me, but the fact remains that she enjoyed the support of a woman who worked as a wife. Our public sense of relationship responsibilities has advanced to the point where a wealthy woman is often required to pay alimony to her former husband if he is not so wealthy. Does any woman owe another woman money on assets accrued while they were together? To expect Martina to be the test case on this issue seems cruel and unusual punishment, but someone had to be first—although I guess that honor belongs to Billie Jean King.

No one of us has the right to judge either Martina or Judy, but I think we can certainly try to understand them.

Let's look first at Martina's world because it shaped her more than she shaped it. Women's tennis created an independent pro tour in the early 1970s. This was perceived as a feminist epipha-ny. Yet the reality of the tour was and remains that players are packaged and marketed if not as latter-day Shirley Temples, then as retro-women. The tour's obsession with femininity in the cosmetic sense is ludicrous.

Competition, still regarded as a male prerogative, must be softened with lipstick, jewelry, pom-poms on the socks, and voices so high-pitched only a dog can hear them. Tennis is a game where one attempts to overpower an opponent either physically or through superior strategy. For women's tennis to try and counterbalance this "masculine" pursuit by false femininity is a masterpiece of wishful thinking.

To carry this notion to its logical conclusion, women's tennis ought to disengage from Virginia Slims as a sponsor and peddle designer diaphragms.

Martina deserves a great deal of praise for never subscribing to the tendril school of coiffure or appearing on court with so much green eyeshadow that she resembled a shrimp gone bad. She wore the required skirt, picked up her racket, and demolished her opponent as a true athlete. Gender was irrelevant.

But strong as Martina was on court, she couldn't always ignore her treatment off court. You would have thought she was the Ogress of the Game because she was a lesbian—not that she admitted it, but neither did she deny it, except for one brief, unshining moment when she gave a press conference in August 1981 with Nancy Lieberman, former basketball star. The gist of this conference was that Nancy was leading Our Heroine back to men. This dedication and sacrifice to the purity of heterosexuality must have been quite overwhelming to those who knew Martina. I have often wondered what credentials one must have to induce a leopard to change her spots. Despite Nancy's sacrificial toils in the lists, Martina soon relapsed into the arms of Judy Nelson.

Having made this brave try with her former friend only proves how subtle and corrosive the attitude on tour was, to say nothing of the attitude in society at large, which is actually more liberal than within the tour. Still, the urge to conform, to be free of the silent censure—if only for a little while—had to be potent. Small wonder that when Martina did fall deeply in love, it was with a woman who exemplified, who was the apotheosis of, the beautiful American wife and mother.

If Martina couldn't be that woman and receive that heterosexual privilege, she could be involved with one.

Imagine living day in and day out in an environment where the mere mention of lesbianism enshrouds everyone in a cloud of ornate gloom. The public will turn away from women's tennis.

We'll lose our sponsors. Etc. Etc. Etc. The histrionics surrounding lesbianism are worthy of the theater. Are there Tonys for hypocrisy?

The reasons that Martina today has been transformed into a legend of the game is not because anyone is experiencing lobal warming. It's because once and for all she has said who she is, period. There's no point in the powers-that-be pretending otherwise. They don't mention it, but they are relieved of the burden of disproving it.

They also know Martina will soon be out of the game, so what does it cost them to respect and adore her now? Then, too, she has made so much money for everyone that a few of them have realized—accummulating knowledge at a glacial rate—that she really is worthy of respect. Coming at long last from inside tennis and the media, this must be a melancholy exultation for Martina.

Martina's world is exceedingly narrow, so narrow that those in charge of tennis fail to observe that the great female star of the younger generation is Madonna, a genuine gender-bender. They are as out of touch with current America as the Republican administration that was handed a resounding, thundering defeat in November 1992. It is a world in which lesbianism is the ultimate horror, whereas sexual congress between a coach and his/her vastly younger charge is tolerated—not publicized, but tolerated. It is also a world in which the financial exploitation of a child physically pushed to compete by a parent is also tolerated although again nothing is ever admitted publicly, but those offenders seem to be perceived as less destructive to the game (read: the market) than two adult women who are in love.

We have all come to accept the Machiavellian schism between morality and politics. Apparently we are now to accept that gulf between morality and sports. Small wonder that Martina's moral compass wavers.

Judy's world exists in sharp contrast to the world of professional sports, where people come and go and are rapidly forgotten. She was raised to make a commitment and to bulldog it. No letting go no matter what. Drugs. Alcohol. Infidelity. Madness.

You hang in there. Stand by your man. In sickness and in health. For richer or for poorer.

Admirable as that may be on paper, in life such relentless devotion can be suffocating.

If sports values people only insofar as they are able to bring in the crowd (read: money), then those Texas belles are valued for running a home, wearing "serious" hair, never raising their voices, and smiling through. The reward for this behavior, for being Mother Cabrini, Hazel the maid, a Grace Kelly socially and a harlot in bed—and all at once, mind you—is that you will be loved, not just loved but LOVED. This is the crown of your existence, the unswerving devotion of your man, the admiring cheers of your friends, and deference from the community. For you have justified their lives.

It should also be noted that love carries a price tag. Men, should they marry one of these female paragons, pay the price for love and then they pay the tax, too. A man chosen by such a lady—and the lady always chooses the man despite appearances to the contrary—knows that he had better damn well keep her. If such a wife were a horse, I would say "not an easy keeper." Appearances cost, social cachet is expensive. Once out of his twenties, the husband of such a beauty realizes, consciously or unconsciously, that his wife's ornamental value reflects directly his own masculine value. To have a beautiful wife and not surround her with beautiful things isn't as bad as castration, but it runs a close second. People whisper behind their hands, sometimes you can even hear them titter. After a while it doesn't even matter whether you love her or she loves you, the marriage, the team, you could even say the Partnership—with the man as General Partner, of course—has a market value. Appearance overtakes substance. The mistress soon follows—but, wouldn't you know it?, she's expensive, too.

Never underestimate the incredible pressure an upper-middle-class man or an upper-class man is under to present a suitable wife. It also helps if the children are blond and blue-eyed.

The wife tirelessly works for the betterment of those less

fortunate than herself. Lest you think I am mocking them, I'm not. If those women didn't do their charity work, the thin veneer of concern for others would evaporate with one hot breath from an accountant.

She also tirelessly works to maintain her looks. If you want to see some scared women, hang out in Houston, Beverly Hills, or Palm Beach and watch those girls hit forty.

The children must attend the right schools—never public schools. One really ought to be an Episcopalian, but mavericks can occur. I knew a Methodist once. The appropriate country club is a dire necessity—and be careful where you vacation. You wouldn't want to relax with people of an inferior social class.

Naturally, you never ever admit any of the above. The hypocrisy is so natural that it's not even hypocrisy—it's good manners.

Judy comes from this rigid, "proper" world. What's ironic is that no one on the East Coast ever considers anyone from Texas to have "papers." They are perceived as nouveaux riches or, as an aunt once said to me about the Reagans, "There's a lot to be said about being nouveau riche, and the Reagans mean to say it all." As she is in her nineties, I suppose she's earned her prejudices, but it is this prejudice that probably makes Texans so vulnerable in their attempts to have "class." They will never figure out that bloodlines count for more than the money, and I, personally, love that about them. The air on the East Coast is sometimes so thin you need an oxygen mask. In Fort Worth you can breathe.

But Judy didn't only come from this world, she was its star, the Maid of Cotton, sent to the court of LBJ. Her wedding was the Fort Worth version of Prince Charles and Diana. She did everything right. Everyone told her so, too. In her own way, she was as praised for her exploits as Martina was praised for her tennis. Martina had athletic prowess. Judy had beauty. They are the lesbian version of Marilyn Monroe and Joe Dimaggio—only Joe got fed up.

Nothing in Judy's background prepared her to see life as anything but a well-decorated set, with herself like Loretta Young, swooping down the curving stairway. Even if something a little off-color happened—like infidelity—why, you loved your way through it and probably changed your hair color in the bargain.

You prayed God to forgive your sins because if you'd been really, really perfect, Mr. Right wouldn't have strayed in the first place. For whatever reason, God doesn't do too good on infidelity; but then, again, he is a male God. They all stick up for one another.

The real issue may be that monogamy is not terribly realistic, or as I often say to my friends struggling with this problem, "Monogamy is contrary to nature but necessary for the greater social good." We're each left to forge our own answer.

Judy's answer was to be more perfect, to work harder. Two great blows had to befall her before she questioned the system itself. Until then she shouldered the blame. But isn't that how we're trained: to see problems as personal instead of institutional or systemic?

The first crack in the facade was her husband's roving eye. The second blow was thrown when she fell in love with Martina. In the time it takes to kiss another human being she was robbed of her individuality on yet another level. Even as she discovered a dimension to herself that made her more complete, the world in which she lived dehumanized her.

Were people vile to her face? No, those kinds of people listen to Pat Buchanan. What she experienced was the subtle and corrosive homophobia that judges lesbian experience negatively. For example, a heterosexual plays the field. The lesbian or homosexual is said to be promiscuous. A heterosexual, uncoupled, is waiting for Mr. or Ms. Right. The lesbian is perceived as being unable to make a commitment. A heterosexual woman is charming. A lesbian is manipulative. A heterosexual woman in love with an older man engages in a December-May relationship. A lesbian in love with an older woman is looking for a mother. If she is older, she's making up for not having children. A beautiful heterosexual woman is celebrated. A beautiful lesbian is told, "What a waste." An unattractive heterosexual woman is often presented as having a good personality or being well groomed.

Some attempt is made to be kind. An unattractive lesbian is a lesbian because she can't get a man. A heterosexual couple marrying is wished good luck, and their community assembles to cherish the bond. Two women making a lifelong commitment are told it won't last.

The truly ignorant still think that a woman is a lesbian because of a man in her life. Something went wrong. The shocker is that a woman is a lesbian because of a woman. It has nothing to do with a man, and I suppose the male ego is such that even when men are out of the game completely, they need to think that a woman is responding to them negatively. It's funny, although I don't see too many men laughing at themselves over this one.

But everything and anything having to do with a bond between two women is seen or presented in a twisted or negative light. A straight woman with a temper is described as having a hair-trigger temper. A lesbian with a temper is hot-tempered because she is a lesbian. All behavior is perceived as deriving from the lesbianism.

The fundamental oppression for a lesbian is that she is denied her individuality. All subsequent mistreatment rests on that foundation.

Imagine the profound impact on Judy Nelson, Maid of Cotton, wife and mother, when the people who knew and loved her so long as she conformed to their ideal suddenly saw her in a less-than-flattering light. She was damaged goods.

Martina built her armor over the years to overcome the slings and arrows of lesbian misfortune. Her winnings helped considerably. But—money or not—she was put in the position of grappling with the shock of a woman who had been a star and, instead of receiving roses, was ducking tomatoes.

Judy went into the relationship, in her mind, under the same terms that she married Ed. She didn't know there was a different way to be in a relationship and, truth be told, Martina needs a wife. If that word rattles your fillings, then how about primary support person? That's got the ring of psychobabble to it. At any rate, a professional athlete might be dazzled by an artist, another athlete, or a business powerhouse. Dazzle doesn't translate into a day-by-day relationship. If you want someone to travel with you and minister to you, then he or she must forgo his or her former life and pack his or her suitcases and yours.

And what does a woman or man get for this? Love. That word again. Jewelry, houses, and cars help, too, but who owns them? Who earned them? How were they earned? Was it a joint effort?

If you know the two women, it's easy to see how the end of the relationship focuses sharply on their differences and their expectations. Judy made a bargain: the bargain of the heterosexual woman. The two women signed an agreement over resources and even made a videotape concerning their separation should the dread day ever occur. Well, it did, and it brought each person's hidden values to the surface.

Not even a well-funded public relations push by Linda Dozeretz on Martina's behalf could completely obscure the core of the disagreement: what does one woman owe another?

The paradox of the divorce, if you will, was that Judy had become enough of an individual to fight back. The experience of loving another woman forced her to examine not just herself, but her entire society. Even as society sought to strip her of her individuality, she found her true self. Some of that is the direct product of nearly a decade with Martina.

As for Martina, she also had to examine many issues—not the least of which is that she has been managed, at times coerced, other times cajoled, into positions she doesn't truly believe by those who say they love her, by those whose bread and butter depends on her winning tournaments. Is there anyone out there who likes her for herself, or must she win tournaments, pay the bills? Is she a real person or a money machine? To be thirty-six years old and experience disillusionment when she ought to be basking in the glow of hard-won comfort can't be a happy experience. Unfortunately, Martina won't know who her real friends are until she is about forty-five. By that time there won't be any more celebrity appearances to squeeze out of her remarkable frame. I hope she can wait that long.

What will become of Martina and Judy in terms of their relationship?

First, let me tell you that I am not a romantic. Literature is divided between romantics and classicists. I am a classicist. In everyday life, the dividing line is between heart and head. Let's just say that I like to think things through.

Two women shared an intense eight years together. They loved one another, with precious little help from anyone around them. They made their mistakes. Who doesn't? When their relationship ended, each woman was quite consistent with her background's approach to such a problem: Judy was taught to hang on and, should the worst happen, then to secure her financial future. A woman of a certain age, alone, is in a precarious position.

Martina's father left her and her mother flat. Sometimes he'd come around, but not often. Done is done, and you get on with your life. Nobody gives anybody anything. Hell, under Communism, the responsibility of the individual is corrupted deliberately by the state. You watch out for yourself, say whatever "they" want to hear, and do the best you can.

It will take both Martina and Judy years to figure out what happened, why it happened, where they were contributors to their own pain, and where they really were right.

But neither one can wipe out those years. There's no question that they gave one another a great deal emotionally, and each one will draw on that capital for the rest of their lives.

Will they find their way back to a less volatile relationship, a friendship on new terms? Yes. I know that Martina swears she will never be friends again with Judy, but I believe I know Martina better than she knows herself. She's been wounded, she's never had to fight a battle like this with any former amours, and she's still dazed by it. She'll get over it. She's impulsive, generous, loving, and adventuresome. She's not going to cave in and whine for the rest of her life about Judy and the money. Everyone's got their hands in her pockets anyway; it's a way of life.

Judy was direct about the relationship and demanded something for those years. Ultimately, Martina will see that demand as a chance to examine her own submerged beliefs about love. What we say about love and what we do about love are generally two different things. If it were not so, would divorce be the spectator sport that it is? Every relationship is loaded with hidden assumptions. For Martina the hidden assumptions came out of the closet. That's a gift.

But far more and far deeper, there will be some moment years from now when Martina remembers something tender—a song, maybe, or a place will bring back the moment. She'll work her way back to a friendship in good time, when the people around her who have something to gain by flogging Judy as the Great Gold Digger are out of her life. Martina will eventually learn that life is too short to jettison eight years of love. Not even Martina is rich enough to buy back time.

Judy could try to work toward a relationship now. Not that it would be easy, because Judy, the bulldog, will want to know how, why, when and where, and just exhaust Martina with her need for answers.

There really are no answers. Love is, by definition, irrational. To submit it to rational criteria irritates everyone and makes matters worse. Instead of trying to find out "what she did wrong" or "what Martina's issues are," Judy just has to accept that these things happen. Period. She can't just assign emotions to Martina and tell her what she's feeling. She must also hear whatever her former partner tells her; today that wouldn't be very salutary. But tomorrow, or the next day, or next year, Judy will be able to accept Martina for who she is—not for the woman who let her down.

If they can't ever become friends, it will be a loss to each of them. Who knows you better than your ex? Whatever attracted you to that person initially is still there. No one can fool anyone for eight years, so there's a lot of good in these two women and a lot of good they have left to give one another.

In the meantime, they will both get on with the soap opera that is daily life, as will you and as will I. I hope everyone's got a good script!

Roger, Wilco, Over and Out.

Rita Mae Brown

Preface

In 1990 I watched Martina Navratilova win her record ninth singles title at Wimbledon. I was seated behind the Royal Box, directly behind Johnny Carson. As Martina ran into the stands to embrace Judy Nelson, I turned to my friend and said, "I know this sounds strange, but it looks like a farewell embrace to me." I didn't think about it again until I read in *USA Today*, in February 1991, that Martina and Judy had separated. And then, not again until I met Judy Nelson, by chance, in Aspen in June.

For years it had been my practice to attend Grand Slam tournaments when possible and to attend the U.S. Open annually. I had spent fifteen years of my life in a dance studio and had a special appreciation of Martina's grace and elegance on the court as well as her discipline and dedication. I had no idea that I was actually following a story that would one day be written in my voice. It has always seemed to me that following what is compelling to your heart eventually leads to productivity.

When Judy asked me to write her story with her, I jumped in with both feet. I thought myself a good candidate for the task because I felt I understood the issues in the case, I understood the game of tennis, and I trusted myself to tell the reader the things I found most interesting about Judy and Martina.

This book evolved from a narrowly focused work covering the events surrounding the *Nelson* v. *Navratilova* case, to a book about Judy's conversion experience, Martina's life on and off the court, the raising of two young men in a divided family, a family's support for one another, and a feminist perspective on family law in Texas. All were pieces of the puzzle and, as such, they needed to be included.

While I entered the case on Judy's side, I was suspicious of the Hill and Nelson families. I, too, had read tales of greed and conspiracy. The Hills and Nelsons allowed me into their homes and answered all my questions. They cried when they talked about Martina, and before long, I was convinced that they loved her.

I was surprised by Eddie and Bales. I didn't expect to enjoy them. In fact, it was my intention (and protective nature) to leave them out of the story whenever possible. However, stories have a life of their own, and the boys turned out to be the most honest and genuine part of this one.

My task was to present the reader with both sides of the story. I did this to the best of my ability. It would be irresponsible of me, as a sociologist, not to mention several assumptions under which I work. First, I believe that structure often dominates interaction and that facts are constructed socially. I believe that we are products of our class origin and class standing and that our "personalities" are a composite of these and other social conditions. I mention this by way of telling you that I do not believe either side was malicious or calculating and that I do believe that both women are products of their very different environments. I believe the legal process caused them to reconstruct their separate and polarized interpretation of the "facts." I believe we all construct and interpret the events that surround our own lives in the same manner. William Faulkner was right when he observed, "Facts and truth have little to do with each other." And, finally, you should know, whenever possible, I reverted to the wisdom that says, when the truth contradicts the legend, go with the legend.

After spending eighteen months focused on Judy and Martina, I am left with several lasting impressions. First, I believe that when their relationship was good, it was very good. I believe that the best predictor of future behavior is past behavior. I now understand the reason seasoned biographers usually have the good judgment to write their works after the deaths of their subjects; then their responsibility is solely to their readers. Mine was not.

My editor had the good sense to insist that I include juicy tidbits that he insisted would enrich this "human-interest story," and I thank Allan Wilson of Carol Publishing Group for his patience and tenacity.

I am grateful to Judy for giving me the opportunity to work with her. Clearly, without her trust and friendship, I could not have written her story. I appreciate the professional manner in which Martina has dealt with me. I hope that when the last court battle is over, we will be able to jump over the net and shake hands. As a result of researching this book, I know more than I ever wanted to know about her private life. For the record, I found her generosity and gentleness a wonder.

As a rookie, I asked for and received a good deal of support from my agent, my editors, and my friends. Thank you to Bill Bruns, for editing an unpunctuated, misspelled stack of unorganized material and organizing them into chapters. His experience as a sportswriter was invaluable to me. His optimism, gentleness, and his ability to get the material out quickly were a huge contribution both to the book and to my personal well-being.

Julie Popkin, my literary agent, had the ambitious task of selling the manuscript of a first-time author. Fortunately, I was able to ride in on the back of a news story, but a story does not write itself into a book. More than anyone else, Julie combed through the manuscript for contradictions and spelling errors (more than once threatening to expose my awful spelling errors to the outside world). For your countless hours, thank you.

Thank you to David Island for giving me my first job as a trial behavior consultant.

Thank you to Professor Kristen Luker of the University of California, Berkeley, for her comments and suggestions on the early draft of the proposal, and for getting me into the doctoral program in sociology at Stanford University. And, once there, for reminding me that some people are there to earn the degree, while others simply grab the skills and run with them.

Thank you to Sargent and Frances Hill. You were charming and gracious, always making our relationship more important than my research.

Thank you to my personal assistant, Andy Wolverton, for helping me make impossible deadlines.

This book would not have been possible without the support of my close friends, Anita, Patty, Teramota, Nancy, and Phylis. And finally, thanks to the friends I made along the way: Bonnie, Chantal, Hope, M.A., Philippe, and Sandy.

San Francisco, California
December 6, 1992

On November 21, 1988, in a codicil to their wills, Martina and Judy envisioned the end of their relationship:

Martina and Judy both wish to be buried on the Castle Creek land in Aspen side by side. The small gold bands that they wear on their left hands should be on their fingers.

Be Happy — Life is very good.
We love you.

Martina Navratilova
Judy Nelson

Love Match

1

The Introduction

"Mom, this is Martina. Martina, this is my mom," Eddie said. Eddie is my older son. He is twenty-two years old now, but when that fateful introduction occurred, he was a boy of eleven.

It was the early spring, March 1982, when Eddie was serving as one of the ball boys for a doubles match at the Bridgestone World Doubles Championships, which were held that year in Fort Worth, Texas. With his shiny flaxen hair and his precious smile, he was a charmer. He was always comfortable with adults and found Martina to be a champion who loved children. They became instant friends, and Eddie thought, knowing how much I loved tennis (I played almost every day), that I would like to meet her. He was right. She played the style of game that I admired. She attacked the net constantly, and it seemed my nature to do that, too.

I had taken up the game a few years earlier as part of therapy, an outlet for my emotions. (My husband had told me that he was leaving me to marry a nurse whom he had met at the hospital while he was doing his residency in internal medicine.) As an escape from the troubles I faced at home, I focused a lot of attention on tennis. I not only loved the game, but I felt supported and loved by the friends I made while playing doubles on the club team. As a matter of fact, it was because of this love of the game that my friends and I volunteered to help with the tennis tournament in which Martina was the star. I had trained the ball girls and boys for the event, a first for me. The kids were enthusiastic, especially Eddie. He was bright and eager and an exceptional athlete. He had a long attention span and a very accurate throwing arm, even at that age. Because of this, he was selected to be a ball boy for Martina's match. She had a reputation for being fun with kids. She expected perfection from them when she played a match. The reason for her high standards, I believe, was that any little thing that was wrong, like a delay, or ball being at the wrong end of the court when she was ready to serve, was a distraction, and Martina needed to be focused on the court. Any disruption could cause her to lose the match. The tournament took place in the Will Rogers Coliseum in my home town of Fort Worth, Texas. Martina would be teaming up with her longtime doubles partner, Pam Shriver. And, more important, my son Eddie would have made an introduction to two women, who, two years later, would begin an extraordinary love story.

Who knows what part fate plays in our lives? This meeting was the first and last time that the Bridgestone tournament would ever be held in that town, and it was the last time I ever trained ball kids. When I met Martina, I instantly felt a bond with her, that feeling that this person will be in your life forever. It was a feeling. Unexplained. Accepted.

It was a brief meeting, just as Martina was going on to the court to play a match. But she said that she would see me afterward in the Players Lounge.

She was easy to talk with and she had a great smile and quick wit. She could recall a joke and tell it as well as a stand-up comedian. Her hair was soft brown with some blond highlights. And her body was the best I had ever seen. It was not the sleek body that epitomizes the "southern beauty queen," but a slender, athletic body with well-defined muscles, smooth and tight. There was not an ounce of fat on her. Her legs were to die for, and she had the prettiest hands I had ever seen. I noticed them when I first shook her hand. The skin was soft and flawless, and her grip was firm. I admired the way she shook my hand and looked me right in the eyes.

I was taller than she by two inches. When I stood next to her, I was amazed that I hovered above her. Having seen her on television many times, I thought she was much taller. As it turned out, we wore the same size clothes, and in the years to come, we often shared our clothing with each other.

When we met, my hair was long and had a rather reddish tint to it, and although I am often described as a blonde, my hair is actually auburn. I was tan that spring from having played a lot of tennis, and I had just returned from my annual family ski trip to Colorado. I even remember what I was wearing the day I met her: a bright orange silk blouse and a pair of blue gabardine pants.

We talked for about fifteen minutes, covering such topics as skiing, tennis, and my children. It was getting late, and I had to get Eddie, find my youngest son, Bales (who was nine), and my husband Ed (he never married the nurse), and go home. The next day would begin early as I tried to get the family up and fed and back to the coliseum for the finals.

Martina and Pam won the tournament. After the award presentation, Martina took the microphone and personally thanked me for the great job I did with the boys and girls. It was a full house, and many of my friends were there that day. I was a little embarrassed at being singled out for praise, but at the same time I was proud. I was amazed that she did that.

We had only a brief moment after the ceremony to speak and say goodbye. We were formal and courteous, exchanging words back and forth. But I knew this was a special friendship—one that would not be forgotten. We exchanged phone numbers and addresses, and off she went with her trainer, Nancy Lieberman, to play in yet another tournament. It was her gypsy way of life.

At the time of this first meeting in 1982, I was married to Dr. Ed Nelson, a specialist in internal medicine. We had been married for fifteen years. The first ten had been filled with the victories and struggles, the highs and lows of young love—of two young people fresh out of college embarking on a new and independent life together. I worked—was a pioneer of sorts in the restaurant business, a field filled with men. Not only did I own a Bonanza restaurant, I also ran it. I was an entrepreneur. I hired and fired workers, cooked and cleaned when the help didn't show, and often spent eighteen hours a day making my franchise consistently one of the top ten in sales in the nation. And, by doing so, I put Ed through medical school.

We had our first child, Eddie, during that time. I took my baby to work with me. I had a baby bed and a playpen in my office. I didn't have help at home. There was no nanny. But my parents, Sarge and Frances Hill, were nearby and willing to help in time of need. This would prove to be a trait that would be forever present in my life. My family would always be there to help, no matter what happened in my life.

My husband spent long hours at Parkland Hospital in Dallas, while I was working at the restaurant. He was often on call for long stretches of time—up to seventy-two hours. He was devoted to his patients and committed to his work.

We both worked hard. I believed in Ed. I believed that surely someday all of our hard work would be rewarded and that we would live a comfortable, sophisticated, and happy life together. After all, I was married to the man of my dreams—handsome, intelligent—and I was a successful businesswoman and an energetic mother of two beautiful children. In time I would become the epitome of the professional woman and homemaker.

But the dream of my ideal marriage was shattered after ten years when, on an ordinary evening in November 1977, Ed made a startling announcement. He rose from his desk, came into our bedroom, and said, "I am leaving."

I asked him, "Where are you going?" I was certain he must have gotten a call from the hospital.

But, to my complete surprise, he said, "I am leaving *you*. I have to go now."

I was devastated. I had no idea that he was unhappy. I never thought that Ed would want to leave me. But just one month before he was to finish his residency in internal medicine and go into private practice, he did just that. He left.

Ed filed for divorce the following week. We remained separated for two years. We saw each other, talked, and even dated each other during our separation. We continued to struggle to find some way to repair the damage. Although we tried to push it aside, the stress was forever present.

Our sons were five and three when we first separated. The three of us stayed in the family home while Ed rented an apartment. He was also seeing a psychiatrist at this time. Occasionally I was asked to join his sessions. While I understood Ed's need to work things out, I felt isolated from him. Consequently, I directed my time and my attention to my sons. A bond was formed among the three of us that remained strong and unusually special—a connection that eventually carried us through the most trying of times.

I found out during this two-year period of "trying to hold the marriage together" (because I loved Ed and believed that families should stay together—which is what I had been taught to believe) that Ed had been unfaithful. Not only did he have a girlfriend when he left me that night—one whom he intended to marry—but he had had at least five other extramarital affairs before that one. The fairy-tale world I had always believed in had come to a complete end. I would never, ever be the same. Ed refused to discuss the affairs; I could never find out what caused him to be repeatedly unfaithful. However, much to our credit, we tried to get the marriage back on track.

During the separation, Ed waffled back and forth between wanting to confirm his commitment to me and wanting his freedom. After two years of Ed's "sitting on the fence," unable to divorce me or to marry the nurse, I cross-filed for divorce. I knew I had to get on with my life. Ed had to make up his mind—to stay or to go—and if he couldn't do that on his own, I would force the issue. Ed came home. Although we worked hard on opening up to one another, I can see in retrospect that we failed at communication. We were unable to show our anger or discomfort on any constructive, productive level.

I tried to become "the total woman," to be what I thought Ed wanted. In the process, I lost sight of my own goals and of the equality that I had sought all my life. I was doing what I thought was best for Ed and my family, but I wasn't doing what was best for me. I know now that I could not have given anyone the best *me*.

Martina allowed me a chance to find the equality that I was searching for. I thought this new relationship would allow me a chance to have my own voice. But I made the mistake of falling back on old patterns. I did too much and tried to control things that were not mine to control. Rather than taking control of my own life, I put my needs after hers. I allowed myself to again become the "woman behind the spouse." It couldn't have been good for her, either. There must be a point where the nurtured person in the relationship feels burdened by the nurturer's sacrifices.

I see things differently now. I know I must take care of myself first, and that this is not selfishness. Instead, that is the only way to give the best self you can. I will struggle with this concept all my life. Sometimes I get it right, sometimes I forget and backslide. But I think I'll always be acutely aware that it is a problem that I have. I see this realization as progress.

Ed and I ended our two-year separation in 1979. When I met Martina in 1982, our marriage had been pieced together, although I was still damaged by the mistrust created by Ed's philanderings. I found out that Ed continued to see his nurse-girlfriend for two years after our reconciliation. He revealed to me that he was still seeing the "other woman" and that he had promised again to marry her. I was so devastated that I became numb. He told me that he didn't know why he was still seeing her secretly and that he really didn't want to leave me again. Like the good woman, wife, and mother that I was taught to be, I forgave him and allowed him to stay. After that, the girlfriend was out of his life forever. She moved to California and, to my knowledge, never returned to Texas.

Although she was gone, the damage was done. I continued to try to improve our marriage. I thought I was superwoman and that I could put all these things behind me. I wrapped myself in denial and played my part. But inside I was dying. At home I performed my duties, but the joy and laughter were gone. I believe that trust is a large part of love and, with it gone, I would never truly feel loved—I would never be the same.

But in 1984, when I met Martina for the second time (after not seeing her for two years), I wanted a friend. I wanted to laugh again. I wanted to trust. I wanted intimacy and equality. I no longer wanted to compromise my ideals. I knew that I was no longer in love with Ed. I had made attempts to talk to him, and even mailed a card to his office—one of those you buy at the card shop that somehow tells the person to whom you are sending it that you miss him and you are lonely. I don't remember the exact words, but the sentiment was of that sort. I do, however, remember exactly what I said. I wrote that I was scared because I didn't think I was in love with him anymore, and I hadn't thought that would ever happen to me. I said that I didn't know what to do. This was just two months before I had lunch with Martina in 1984—a lunch that would mark the beginning of a most special relationship and, shortly thereafter, the beginning of a most special love story.

The Beginning

Although they exchanged Christmas cards and spoke on the phone a couple of times, not until March 1984 did Martina and Judy spend any time together. It would take two years for their schedules to allow a lunch meeting; it seemed as though each time Martina was in town on tour, in Dallas or Fort Worth, Judy was away with her family, skiing in Colorado.

After winning the Virginia Slims Championship tournament in New York on March 4, against Chris Evert in three sets, Martina headed to Texas, where she was scheduled to play the Virginia Slims of Dallas. While in town, before the tournament began, Martina asked Judy to lunch. Recognizing this as an unusual opportunity to meet with this fascinating woman, Judy accepted the invitation. At this point Judy had heard rumors that Martina was gay, but she didn't really pay much attention to them. "People would ask me, 'Is Martina gay?' and I would reply, 'Beats me,' " Judy admits.

After Martina's practice, Judy followed her to the house of Mike Epstep, Martina's coach, where Martina showered and put on jeans and a shirt. Then, in separate cars, they drove to the Wyndam Hotel in Dallas, where they ordered chicken-salad sandwiches. Over an uninterrupted and intimate two-hour lunch, they quickly revealed their philosophies, passionate interests, and political views. The conversation was lively, each displaying her wit and humor. They talked about their lives and their loves. By the time they finished lunch, Judy was beginning to experience feelings for Martina that shocked her. "Surely," she thought, "I can't be experiencing this kind of attraction for a woman. I've never felt like this for a girlfriend before—such a confusing kind of excitement."

When they asked for their check, they were informed that the man across the room had already taken care of it. Obviously, their energy could be felt several tables away. Although Judy was a married woman with two young sons—to her surprise, she found herself swept off her feet by Ms. Navratilova. Martina's quick wit and gentle vulnerability were as seductive as they were charming. Judy was both confused and compelled by her attraction to Martina. When they walked out to the parking lot to get in their cars, Martina gave Judy a kiss on the cheek. Judy wasn't clear about its meaning, and it left her even more confused. Martina said she would call Judy and that they would get together again in the next day or two.

Upon Judy's return home that afternoon, she phoned a psychiatrist friend and said, "Karen, I need to see you on a professional basis, because either I'm going crazy or I'm going to be the most interesting case you've had in a long time." Before long, the entire family would have talks with this psychiatrist.

But, for now, this lunch marked the beginning of the romantic relationship between Judy and Martina. Judy, while caught up in the changes, was still married, and neither woman was clear about what this all meant to their lives, so they thought it best to keep their feelings for each other a secret.

During tennis practice that morning, before their lunch, Martina had pulled her hamstring. The injury was quite serious—so serious, in fact, that she was not able to play or compete for over a month. Martina was forced to withdraw from several tournaments, yet what started out as an unfortunate event actually provided Judy and Martina with a window of time in which they grew to know each other. For a while, they could remain suspended, without the pressure of the outside world making demands on Martina's time and energy. For the moment, they could embrace their denial about the pain they would eventually cause the people whom they loved; and the pain they themselves might suffer as they struggled to accommodate each other's needs and demands—needs that could not always be met, and demands that came with the complications of family, especially Judy's children, and public life.

When Judy and her husband Ed realized that Martina would be unable to play for a while, they invited her to stay with them. They offered her Bales's room upstairs. As Judy described the situation, "Martina was just a normal houseguest. She would come and sit down and have dinner with us. Sometimes she would cook dinner, pasta or something, and everybody liked what she fixed." Because the family was focusing on the fact that they were hosting a tennis celebrity, no one paid very much attention to Martina and Judy's relationship. "I wasn't uncomfortable being at the dinner table with Martina, Ed, and the boys. I was just glad she was there. It was easy to be around her. It wasn't that complicated yet. I just wanted to be around her and, if that was the only way we could do it, we would make it work."

Martina had made her way into Judy's heart, and she was now in her home. Martina and Judy had known each other only for a few hours when Martina's injury occurred. Perhaps, had the two been thinking more clearly, they might have chosen a different time and a better place for their beginning; but, as it turned out, Martina was the Nelsons' houseguest, and Judy and Martina grew closer to each other as they experienced everyday life at home together. Somehow, this domestic experience was a great leveler. Judy was in her own environment, and Martina was removed from the tennis world; they were encapsulated in an environment that was perceived by those around them to be one thing, and known by them to be more than others could grasp. In these early days of their relationship, they shared a secret that was meant to be shared—it was just a matter of finding the right time and mustering up enough courage.

Martina's life was in transition. She had some of her things at Nancy Lieberman's house in Dallas and some furniture and clothes were still in Virginia Beach, but she was unsettled and injured. Judy thought the idea of staying with the family appealed to Martina; not only would Judy and Martina be close, but it was also the path of least resistance. At this point, Ed was unaware that Judy had formed a romantic relationship with Martina, and he welcomed the tennis star into their home with open arms. As far as the family was concerned, Martina was simply a houseguest.

Judy and Martina spent the days together getting to know each other. This was the beginning of romance, and they were delighted to be near each other. "We could spend more time together. This was a real getting-to-know-each-other period. We both tried to answer questions, she for herself and me for myself. At this stage there was a definite relationship that had developed, so we had a lot to discuss. What were we going to do about the fact that we were in a relationship? Was she going to leave? What was going to happen to us?" Judy was facing the transition of her life. "We also took time to laugh—something I hadn't done in a long time. Martina would go to the club and watch me play tennis with my friends, sometimes giving me tips on improving my play. She was such fun. All my friends were enchanted. She was easy to be with, and everyone welcomed her."

Judy usually stayed up for several hours each night after the boys and Ed went to bed. Like many mothers, this was a time for reflection which she normally spent alone.

"It was my habit to stay up late at night after everyone had gone to bed. Martina went to bed early each night; but, when she would hear me doing things around the house, she would wake up and then we would spend isolated hours together just sitting and talking about our feelings for each other and where that was leading us and could we make it work. We were both concerned with the effects that the relationship would have on the children and my parents. We knew we needed to be together. You can't just change your life like that. Martina was concerned, too. Her friends were advising her about the problems she would encounter by getting involved with a married heterosexual woman. We talked for hours each night. As I remember, the practical issues were the most important ones. Our discussions were not always romantic."

This went on for about a week, until Dr. Nelson came home from the hospital early one afternoon. Martina had been taking a nap and Judy was sitting beside her on the bed and they were talking about what they would do when Martina had to leave to start playing tournaments again, as the French Open was rapidly approaching. There was certainly nothing romantic going on then, but, just in that moment, Ed understood the electricity between the two. Everyone recognized the moment of truth. The entire room was filled with tension. Judy saw the fear in Ed's face as she looked in his eyes. "I think he sensed it—the feeling in the room that there's something more going on here than friendship. I had told him, months before Martina had entered my life, that I was afraid I wasn't in love with him anymore. Now he knew that I was in love with someone else. I always wore my feelings on my face. I could never really hide anything, nor did I want to. Now, he was truly frightened. I knew it was getting close to the time I had to leave, I could feel the dissolution of our marriage approaching. I didn't know for sure what it was I had to do, but I knew I couldn't live with Ed anymore. I wasn't sure I was going to start living with Martina. I knew that's what I wanted, but having the courage to do it and wanting to do it are two different things."

Judy remembers turning to Ed and saying, "I need to talk to you, and I'll come down to the bedroom in just a minute." She reassured Martina and then, with a heavy heart, she approached the inevitable conversation with her husband.

When Judy joined Ed in their bedroom and sat down beside him, the words didn't come to her easily; she hadn't yet fully defined for herself what was going on. She recalls telling him, "This has been happening, and I don't understand it. But I know our marriage is over, and I am just trying to find my way with this relationship with Martina. I feel in my heart that's what I want, but I don't know how to do it or if I have the courage to do it because there is so much involved."

As Judy spoke to Ed, she became a little more sure of what she needed. She heard herself defining her relationship with Martina, and although this first step of breaking away from him was painful, she felt certain that her feelings for Martina were good and honest, and that she was willing to let go of her heterosexual privilege, knowing that she would gain a special bond with Martina. A bond she felt would last forever.

Ed was devastated and angry. His male ego was threatened. He had no way to compete with a woman—especially one who was rich and famous. He insisted that Martina had to leave. Martina had anticipated this and was eager to pack her bags and head for a nearby hotel, the Green Oaks Inn, on the west side, but still near Judy. For the next few weeks, Martina stayed there while Judy spent most of her days with Martina. Their days together were full, rich, and easy—filled with laughter much of the time. They went on walks and picnics and listened to music. They talked about the possibility of living together and what that would mean to each of their lives. While they separated each night, they were together during the day.

The evenings, however, weren't always easy. During these long nights, Judy often felt the need to create excuses to leave the house for short periods of time, allowing herself to swing by the Green Oaks Inn to visit Martina. She did this when she could think of a good reason to get away, always bearing small gifts such as bagels, sandwiches, or fruit. In these stolen moments, they listened to music and made plans. Perhaps the tantalizing experience of not being able to see each other during the evening enriched their days together. As each day passed, Judy's desire to be with Martina grew more compelling, and there was less and less room for fear. It wasn't easy leaving Martina in the hotel room alone, but Judy needed to sort things out with Ed and the boys.

Meanwhile, Martina was gradually recovering from her hamstring injury and had begun training for a tournament on Amelia Island, off Florida—the Women's Tennis Association Championship, April 16 to 22. She was joined by Judy midweek, who flew out to see her play for the first time.

"I thought she was awesome," Judy recalls, "But I just didn't realize *how* awesomely she played that week. I didn't know she hated playing on clay. I didn't know the difference between clay and hard courts and grass, the different games and different strategies each require. It was all new to me. And this was Chris Evert's home club at the time, and she had never lost there. When Martina beat Chris, it was one of the happiest moments of her life. She wanted me to share it with her. She was proud of herself and she wanted me to be proud of her, and I was."

Martina displayed the grace of a gazelle and the heart of a lion as she took her place on court. She was engaged with life, and it had a wonderful effect on her game. Her performance level soared, and, displaying her best, she looked like a peacock on court. When Martina is in love, it brings out the best in her game, and everyone in the stands becomes aware that she is smiling at her friends in her player's box and winking; it is a show within a show. Tennis becomes a complex way for Martina to communicate her emotions to the world.

Judy couldn't appreciate the Martina-Evert rivalry at this point. She had followed tennis, but she didn't really understand the strategic differences required by each player on different surfaces. The expression, "Chrissie on Clay," seemed like a nice alliteration, but she didn't understand that Chris's ground strokes were well suited for a slow clay surface, while Martina's game was best on a fast surface like grass or cement. For Martina to be effective on clay, she had to change things that were more comfortable and natural to her game. Her powerful serve, which she followed into the net and then volleyed when playing on grass or hard courts, slowed or bit when it hit clay and forced her to play more balls from the back court. Generally, rallies on clay are longer, and the opponent with the best ground strokes, rather than the best serve or volley, wins.

Martina was delighted with herself after winning the match, but it would be a year or two before Judy could fully appreciate what Martina had accomplished on April 22, 1984. On her worst surface, against her best opponent, after not playing for a month, she beat Chris Evert on clay, at Chris's own club. The score: 6–2, 6–0.

Shortly after her Amelia Island triumph, Martina headed for

Europe to prepare for the French Open, which began on May 28, while Judy returned home for a few weeks. Life for both of them was about to become much more complicated. It was one thing for Judy to be seen at a small domestic tournament where the local press was interested in promoting the tennis event, but quite another at a Grand Slam tournament, where there was worldwide coverage of the event and its players. If Judy were to show up at the stadium at Roland Garros, just outside the city of Paris, television cameras would photograph her in Martina's courtside box, and sports writers from all over the world would take notice. This would not be as it had been in the United States where a faint whiff of a scandal might have simply raised an eyebrow or two among friends in Fort Worth. Ed agreed to let Judy go to Paris. He really had no choice. He had to take the chance that Judy would change her mind and come to her senses. Eddie and Bales were still not aware of the romantic friendship between their mother and Martina, so they thought it was great that their mom was getting to see Martina play in a Grand Slam event.

The French Open is played on red clay courts and is one of four Grand Slam events played during the tennis year. Martina had already won the Australia Open, the United States Open, and Wimbledon the previous year and now had an opportunity to do something extraordinary. If she were to win the French Open (an event she had won only once before), she would capture the Grand Slam title by winning all four events in succession. If sheer glory weren't enough incentive, Philip Chatreau, president of the Tennis Federation, had promised a million-dollar bonus to anybody who could capture the Grand Slam.

This kind of pressure excited virtuoso performances from Martina, who was now at the top of her game. This excitement in her career certainly added to the attraction that Martina and Judy felt for one another and would soon make them appear larger-than-life to audiences around the world. In Paris, they burst on the scene with a particular kind of attractiveness, Martina and Judy were perceived as "wholesome and likable." Judy had softened Martina in a way that added to her popular appeal.

But there were still issues to be resolved at home. Martina had wanted Judy to travel with her to Europe, but Judy knew that her own emotional interests would best be served by returning home, where she could make an honest attempt to iron out family matters without the distractions of a blossoming romance. The painful time at home was spent talking with Ed, trying to decide what she was going to do. She had only those options that seemed real to her, honest choices that were consistent with her emotional needs. She agonized: how could she be with Martina and continue to be a good mother to her sons?

When she returned from Paris, Judy sought the advice of her family minister, Dr. Barry Baily. At first she talked to him herself, and later both she and Martina spoke with him. "We talked about the choice I was making and the social consequences of such a choice. I was filled with such inner distress as a Christian, and I needed the comfort and compassion of my religion, which I got from Dr. Baily. When Martina and I left, I felt that we knew what we were doing and that we were truly happy. He was never judgmental, and he continued to stay in touch with us throughout the years," Judy recalled. As it turned out, Dr. Baily would be called upon to help the entire family with Judy's lifestyle change.

Judy knew that the time had come for her to reveal her plans to her sons. She felt awkward withholding so much of her life from them. She and Ed decided to tell the boys about her relationship with Martina, but not until she returned from France.

Judy arrived at the French Open during the round before the quarterfinals. Martina met her at the airport. They drove to the hotel (Martina always drove her cars herself—she hated to be driven). At the hotel she had wonderful surprises waiting for Judy. Martina had purchased an entire set of Louis Vuitton luggage and a pair of heart-shaped diamond earrings for her. Judy was overwhelmed. The French press noticed Judy in Martina's box with Martina's parents and friends—Mumsey Nemiroff, an art expert from the University of California, Los Angeles, and her husband, Al. For the most part, the relationship had not been made public, which allowed Judy and Martina to keep their secret safely guarded and out of the hands of the world. Yet, off the court, Judy was by Martina's side day and night.

The night after Judy arrived in Paris, she phoned Hot Springs, Arkansas, to talk to Ed and the boys and her parents, Sarge and Frances Hill. "I had just arrived, and I wanted to see how everyone was doing," Judy remembers. To her surprise, the family had been discussing her relationship among themselves. "They were all crying when I called. Ed had told them about Martina and me. And the boys were on the line crying for me to come home. I was angry because Ed had promised to let me tell the boys in my own way. I was torn. My heart was breaking. Martina was sitting next to me in the hotel room, and I knew she wanted me to stay with her. She was in the quarterfinals. But what could I do? My family was devastated. The boys were so young and so hurt. I had to let them know that I was their mother and was not going to abandon them. But the family would have to support each other until I got home. I knew where I had to be; this was an important time in Martina's life. And mine."

Martina sat in the room while Judy talked to her family, witnessed the pain on her face. Judy concluded the conversation with her mother by saying, "I only have a few more days here and you all have each other right now. Hold yourselves together. I love you." Still crying herself, Judy got off the phone and wept with Martina.

While this was very painful for everyone, it was clear that Judy was going to stay with Martina and that Martina could rely completely on her. The choice had been made. Judy recalled, "Martina was going for the Grand Slam. This was huge, and to have all this turmoil obviously would upset her and affect her. . . . This was really a tough thing for us to deal with because she likes to stay focused on her game. And so, here, on clay, a surface that she hates, and with a million-dollar check on top of everything else, the timing of this episode (the telephone conversation) was not good."

Martina advanced to the finals, where she met Chris Evert. In the box, Judy sat with Martina's family. Martina won a decisive straight-sets victory over Chris in the final, 6–3, 6–1.

Martina headed for England to compete in a grass tournament in Eastbourne and prepare for Wimbledon, while Judy headed back to Fort Worth. Martina's warm-up tournament for Wimbledon went well, as she defeated Kathy Jordon 6–4, 6–1, and captured another grass-court victory. Meanwhile, Judy was met at the Fort Worth airport by her parents and children. As they drove up to her house, she could see that the boys had draped a banner between two trees in front of the house. It read, "Welcome Home Mom." "When I drove up and saw that banner, I was filled with emotion for my sons," Judy recalled. "I knew how devastating this was to them. It was as though they were crying out, 'Don't leave us, Mom.' " But even with all this pain, Judy recalled that because of this wonderful relationship with Martina she felt freer and more fulfilled than she had been in her entire life. But because of the way she was raised, being happy in the midst of so much pain caused her to suffer and feel extremely selfish. But she was eager to get on with her new life with Martina.

Judy and Martina talked each day on the phone for hours. The reality of this transition was forced upon her parents and children, and she needed to be with them for a few weeks. Her mother and father pleaded with her to move slowly, to examine her feelings carefully. Judy's mother would tell her that they would die of broken hearts. During this time, Judy's parents talked to their minister about Judy's new lifestyle; they were religious people, and they sought spiritual guidance. Judy remained with her family and tried to answer their fears with care and gentleness. She would speak with them in groups and individually, trying to help them understand her choice and her newfound happiness. They were extremely concerned about social chastisement and the peer pressure the boys would suffer. They were also afraid of the permanent consequences of her choice to be with a woman if Martina should ever leave Judy. They never questioned the fact that Judy might want to leave

Martina. They knew Judy's sense of commitment and loyalty, for they had seen her go through a tumultuous marriage with Ed. Besides, commitment and loyalty is what they had taught her best.

She coddled the boys during her return, not telling them she was leaving to "join" Martina on the tour, giving them time to adjust to her "special friendship," asking them to accept her and to see Martina as an addition to the family, rather than as a catalyst for its destruction. Meanwhile, Martina and Judy were planning a move after Wimbledon. They chose a house that would be finished by the time they returned to the United States in mid-July.

Wimbledon 1984

Judy knew from experience that the best way to deal with confusion and pain in the midst of turmoil was to return to familiar patterns, when possible. So, in mid-June, as summer camp for her two sons approached, Judy wanted to continue a family tradition by making sure that Bales and Eddie were packed properly and then dropped off at summer camp. They needed to know that, although their mother was no longer going to be home every day, many things would remain the same between them. Judy helped pack their trunks, and when she left them off, she promised to return in three weeks to pick them up: dirty socks and all.

Despite Judy's attempts to comfort her sons, she knew she was the one causing their pain. Her gentleness was a reminder of the consistency and security they would soon lose. At the same time, they needed her attention and commitment. Six years earlier, their parents had separated for over two years. They wanted to remain a family, yet they knew their parents' marriage had been fragile for years. Eddie had asked his mother, several months prior to Martina's entrance into her life, "Mom, why are you so much happier at the club with your friends? You laugh all the time. But when Dad comes home, you don't laugh at all."

That one question from her young son said more to Judy about the frailty of her marriage than any other single event. She knew he was right, and she wondered why she had not verbalized it herself. She realized it was because she tried to keep herself so busy with the needs of everyone else that she hadn't had time to reflect on her own.

With the boys cared for and entertained at camp, Judy felt free to return to Europe, where she joined Michael Estep, Martina's coach, his wife Barbara, and Martina at the hotel in Eastbourne. Judy was there to see Martina win the tournament, after which they drove in a silver Porsche (provided for them by the Porsche Co.) to Martina's house in Wimbledon. Not only was Wimbledon played on Martina's favorite surface (she had captured this title four times), but she has always found a certain enchantment with the customs and ceremonies that surround the tour's premier event. Each year the world's finest players are summoned to appear before the British royalty for a magical fortnight of dazzling excitement and civilized tradition. Players still wear all white, and are required and honored to curtsy and bow to the royal box as they enter and exit center court. Martina was in her element, the number-one female player in the world; this was her prime, and she looked and felt confident, untroubled by the insecurities that had haunted her earlier in her career.

In England, the house which Martina traditionally rented is near Court One, just seconds from Wimbledon's All England Lawn Tennis and Croquet Club. Once she and Judy entered the small village near London, they would be under close watch. The world descends upon this tiny village for two weeks each summer, and the village is packed with people who are immobilized, at times, due to the congestion. Wimbledon fans are among the most sophisticated in the world; they know the subtleties of the game and bring with them to the club high expectations of the players' performances—on and off court. They know their heroes and can spot them immediately. Therefore, after having spotted Judy at the French Open, fans and the press were waiting for her arrival.

Following Martina's Eastbourne matches, the early rounds at Wimbledon went well, but perhaps, more important at this stage of her life, she and Judy were feeling hopeful about their relationship. Any lingering doubts they may have experienced in the past about the complexity of their relationship and its viability were gone, and in their minds were dreams and plans about a future filled with loyalty and commitment.

The two women were fast becoming the talk of Wimbledon—a town filled with reporters from every corner of the world. Judy had underestimated the size and devotion of Martina's fans, who wanted to know more about the new woman in her life. Now she would experience the vigor with which the press pursued Navratilova in order to accommodate her fans' curiosity about her private life.

Judy made her Wimbledon debut during Martina's second-round match against Amy Holton. When she arrived, she sat behind Martina's box, to avoid reporters. Martina was behind by one game in the first set when Judy arrived, but she turned her game around quickly and advanced with a 6–2, 7–5 win.

The press proved relentless, and as soon as they spotted Judy in the stands, Martina was asked few questions about her game, but the Fleet Street journalists appeared to be insatiable when it came to her personal life. As far as they were concerned, Judy and Martina provided more juicy tidbits than they could have dreamed possible: a Texas beauty queen and mother of two with the tennis champ.

Suddenly the two were at the center of several intriguing stories. While some viewed their relationship as abnormal, others saw them as folk heroes who were boldly asking the world to accept their relationship as equal to any. As social actors, they were asked to negotiate in the tennis world and in the feminist community. Each domain had specific expectations of them, and they needed to jointly develop skills to address these demands, while building their relationship. For the next few years, Martina and Judy would have to adjust to the social climate of the tennis world, the needs of the press and the hopes of the feminist community.

The London press was persistent, but Judy had been warned about them. When you are coupled with the number-one player in the world, you must be prepared for attention. As players advance through the rounds, they receive more and more coverage. Judy was able to adjust to this attention as long as that kind of sensationalism remained in Europe, away from Texas. However, Frank DeFord, an American reporter for *Sports Illustrated*, wrote an article that caused Judy to feel victimized by careless reporting. He reported that Judy had "thrown a kiss" to Martina from the stands. For the record, it never happened, and it was especially painful because Judy's sons and their friends read about it. Had that sort of thing been confined to the scandal sheets, they would have never seen it and would have been spared the teasing. (Years later, Mr. DeFord and Judy discussed this story at some length. He apologized for hurting the boys, but he insisted that he reported what he thought he had seen.)

As the time came for Judy to leave Wimbledon and fly home to Texas to pick her boys up from camp, she was well aware of how much she did not want to be without Martina. Being on tour together and sharing time away from her family had caused them to develop an even closer bond. Now they were sharing the highs that the professional sports world offers its stars. The contrast between Judy's past and the place where she now found herself was startling. This polarization was too consuming; she couldn't keep up with the emotional demands of Martina and her world, while trying to pretend that things could remain status quo at home. It wasn't fair to anyone involved. She felt she had to shift her loyalty to Martina and find a new way of being a mother to her children. The two could not be mutually exclusive; they couldn't compete with one another. Judy had no model for what she was undertaking, so she had to trust her feelings. She had to remain close to her sons, while giving her loyalty to Martina.

July recalled, "However, Martina was very attentive to my needs at this point in the relationship. She made a personal effort to introduce me to two ladies who had lived together for many years and who at one point in their lives had had to make similar choices and decisions. These ladies became wonderful friends of mine and would prove to be a rock for me in the sometimes turbulent and high-profile, controversial world Martina and I shared. From them, I found that mine was not an isolated case, where a woman in midlife (with children) chooses to live with another woman. For, in the very beginning, I had no one with whom to identify. I was certain that I was the only one in the world who had ever had to face such a dilemma. I was not. And these two women continue to be a source of strength and guidance and love for me."

Martina and Judy had set up a house in Texas (near Ed's) that was being built, but was not yet completed when she left for Wimbledon. The house was on Roaring Springs Road in Fort Worth. During the time she was not on the road, she would remain geographically accessible to her children. This was understood.

In the middle of the Wimbledon matches, Judy flew from Heathrow to Dallas-Fort Worth for about a thirty-hour stay, to pick up the boys from camp—but also to explain to them that she and Martina were going to live together after Wimbledon.

When Ed and Judy drove up to camp in their Bronco, they saw their boys and their campmates, tanned from the Texas sun and all combed and neat for parents' arrival, standing in line, looking for their families to carry them home. They spotted the boys, and together Judy and Ed walked up to them and said, "We missed you guys." Judy then directed them, "Go get the trunks and we'll back the car up and you can load 'em in." They loaded everything in the car and headed for a pizza parlor on the way home. Judy slipped a John Denver tape in the cassette player in the dash of the Bronco, and they were on their way. At the table in the pizza parlor, Bales asked the question that produced the answer he didn't want to hear. In his hopeful nine-year-old voice, Bales asked, "Are you gonna stay home now, Mom?"

"Tears began to run down my cheeks and I could hardly speak," Judy remembered. "The words stuck in my throat. My heart was breaking, and the pain was greater than any I had ever experienced to that point in my life. I had to answer the question. I would tear my family apart and change the direction of my children's lives forever."

It was a difficult and heartfelt conversation for Judy as she confronted her family with the reality that she would be leaving the following morning to begin traveling without them most of the time. This was no time for chatter or small talk. She had come with an agenda, and there was no better time—certainly no good time—to deliver her message. She had only one night to discuss this with Ed and her sons, and she wanted to give the boys as much time that evening as she could. Finally she was able to speak the words that would never be reversed: "No, honey, I'm not." There was only silence as huge tears welled up in the eyes of everyone.

Ed broke the silence by asking the boys to head back to the car so they could discuss this in a private place. Once in the car, Judy began again, saying, "I love you both very much and I know how difficult this is going to be for all of us, but I'm not in love with your father anymore. You know we have both worked very hard for the last seven or eight years to try to keep our marriage together. I cannot do it anymore. I have tried with all my heart, and I have failed."

Eddie was just thirteen at the time. He remembers being extremely angry and deeply hurt. His world was slipping out of his control. He is, and has always been, in the habit of confronting his mother, and others as well. This behavior grows out of a combination of motives; Eddie is emotionally courageous, but often feels dogmatically rational. One is never sure which motive is operating, and it can change on a dime. At this point his motive was clear; he didn't want his family to fall apart. He was operating from honesty and love.

"How could you leave us and Dad? Do you love Martina?"

"Yes, she is my friend and she makes me feel happy. I can even laugh again, Eddie," Judy replied.

But at this point she became overwhelmed with emotion as she looked at their frightened, innocent faces. "I hurt so much for all of us. I know it's not fair. I know you don't understand. I know you're angry. But for some time now I haven't been happy, and I need things to change," she said. Judy assured the boys that she was not leaving them—only Ed—and that she and Ed would share their time with them. She told them that when she was on tour with Martina there would be no need to ask permission—just to let her know when they wanted to be with her, and the travel arrangements would be made. But that is not what they wanted to hear. Much as Judy wanted to break the news as gently as possible, there was simply no easy way to tell two young boys that their mother, whom they had been with constantly from the day they were born, was leaving home to live with another person. They had no way of knowing, in that moment, how she would be accessible to them. They continued their conversation all evening. This was the last night Judy spent with Ed Nelson, her husband of seventeen years.

Ed appeared to be adjusting to the fact that Judy had chosen to live with Martina, but he was angry and protective of his children. "You can go," he told Judy, "but you will never get custody of the boys in Texas." Judy believed and hoped that Ed's position would change over time, and he would allow them the flexibility to freely go from one home to the other. "Ed and I both worked very hard to keep the line of communication open, in order to try and maintain as healthy an atmosphere as possible for the boys. Because divorce had been an option that was discussed many times between the two of us, we knew that we never wanted to fight over custody of the children. We wanted them to feel free to be with either of us whenever they felt the need. We didn't ever want them to ever feel that they had to make a choice of one parent or the other."

While Eddie chose to stay at his father's house, Bales chose to spend most of his time with his mother. This was all right with Ed, but he insisted in the beginning that Judy's parents be present. To accommodate this arrangement, Judy and Martina set up a separate condominium for Judy and the boys and her parents to live in during a six-month transition. While Judy spent her nights at the Roaring Spring house with Martina, her parents stayed at the condo with their grandsons. It was a hardship, but her parents were willing to do more than their share to make sure their daughter and grandchildren could have separate dwelling places but close enough together to retain the family image.

It's amazing how creative you can become when money is not an issue.

The next morning Ed drove Judy to the airport. Before that, she had dropped some clothes and other possessions off at Martina's house, then having taken up residency in their new house, Judy caught a plane and landed in the middle of her new life.

Martina had advanced to the round of sixteen, and before the week was over, there would be reporters from the London papers on the rooftops trying to shoot pictures of Judy and the champ in the kitchen of their Wimbledon house. The press wanted to know all about Martina's new companion.

Of course, not everyone in the tennis world was happy. It has always been the position of the Women's Tennis Association that this kind of publicity is bad for the game, that it reinforces stereotypes about women in sports as though there is a disproportionate correlation. It was no secret that Martina's openness about her sexual preference had cost her endorsements in the past, and this is the kind of negative publicity sometimes used against other women in the sport. It was not unusual to hear a man's voice shout from the stands at critical moments in Martina's matches, "Martina is a dyke." Her honesty about her lifestyle has always been held against her, but her courage in standing up for what she feels is important is appreciated by people all over the world.

Following right behind Judy was a young woman named BeAnn Sisemore, a paralegal working for Jerry Loftin, an attorney who was Judy's personal friend. BeAnn had briefly met Judy six years earlier, when Judy had first filed for divorce through Jerry Loftin's office. Nevertheless, she was now on a mission for Judy's parents and Jerry. They had sent BeAnn over to try to change Judy's decision; they thought BeAnn could convince Judy she was being irrational about her decision to live with Martina. They knew BeAnn had a wonderful sense of humor, was charming and attractive, that she and Judy had similar values, and were both pretty young mothers born and reared in Texas. BeAnn could be a woman Judy respected. But most importantly, BeAnn was an unconditional, solid, dyed-in-the-wool heterosexual feminist.

Arriving in London, BeAnn took one look and said, "You have never looked so happy, Judy." BeAnn's memory of Judy at the time she was filing for divorce from Ed, was that Judy was unhappy and depressed. The Judy she met when she arrived in London was sparkling; she had "I'm in love" written all over her. It didn't take a rocket scientist to conclude that there was little or no chance of Judy returning home. Somehow, real life and a failing marriage didn't hold a candle to this.

Still, BeAnn stayed with Judy and Martina at their house in Wimbledon. One could easily find BeAnn enjoying the matches from Martina's box on center court. After each match, she was eager to attend parties with them. At home in the evening, they all stayed up late at night talking about Judy's new lifestyle. "Martina made BeAnn feel really comfortable. She was open about her feelings. BeAnn knew I was happy and felt very loved and safe with Martina," Judy recalls.

The press mistakenly identified BeAnn for Judy, since they were both Texas blondes. (Texas women having specific Texas hairstyles—usually long, layered, and not their original color. It's not a southern look, or a midwestern look—it's Dallas–Fort Worth, Texas, specific.) Reporters asked her inappropriate questions about her "relationship" with Martina and her husband and children whom she had "abandoned" back home. But BeAnn had a wonderful sense of humor and, despite her best attempt to rescue Judy from a life of sin, she was having the time of her life—and receiving an education that money couldn't buy.

Meanwhile, Martina was advancing toward the finals on her side of the draw, while Chris Evert was doing the same on the other half. As the two were getting set to meet again in the finals, Martina was probably not thinking about her Amelia Island win in late April, nor the French Open triumph, but rather she was perhaps remembering how well Chris played in New York, back in March, at the Virginia Slims final, when they had gone to three sets. Martina had beaten Chrissy 6–3, 5–7, 6–1, but it was a tough match. Chris was mixing up her shots and coming to the net when she needed to, and placing the ball well. With Chris Evert's ability to concentrate, Martina was going to have to be very focused if she was going to depart Wimbledon with a fifth title. Martina was chasing Chris—they had played fifty-nine matches against each other since 1973, and Chris had won thirty of those matches. Martina could catch up to Chris by winning Wimbledon, and they would be tied with thirty match victories apiece.

All that aside, BeAnn had concerns about Judy's financial welfare. What would happen if Martina left her? It was the moment to do some serious thinking about these problems, even in the midst of Wimbledon, before they returned to Texas to start living together. So Martina and Judy talked about making some kind of agreement that would protect them both should anything happen to the other. In the United States, an unmarried woman's estate usually goes to probate; and Judy, without a will and an agreement, would be guaranteed nothing. Judy's chances of successfully defending Martina's will, should Martina's family choose to contest it, would be slim in any state. Martina, on the other hand, could be assured that she would avoid any undue publicity over lawsuits.

Although Judy and Martina had talked about such an agreement when they were in Texas (Martina had scribbled some notes on a piece of stationery from the Green Oaks Inn), this was the first time the idea of a contract—some kind of agreement— surfaced among the three women. It is Judy's recollection that, during a dinner outside in the backyard at Wimbledon, they discussed it calmly among themselves. BeAnn questioned Judy about her decision to abandon the security of her family. True to human nature, when in love, Martina told Judy that she would not have cause to worry; she would take care of her. This marked the inception of the eventual partnership agreement, where all three players were present.

There would later be disagreement between Judy and Martina and BeAnn as to how BeAnn was introduced to Martina. Martina remembers thinking that BeAnn worked *with* Jerry Loftin, rather than *for* him. In other words, that BeAnn was an attorney, representing both Judy and Martina in the development of any kind of agreement. As a paralegal, BeAnn could not fulfill these duties. Later, in court testimony, BeAnn firmly denied that she misrepresented herself to Martina. This distinction about BeAnn's professional status would later play a crucial role when the relationship dissolved and the nonmarital cohabitation agreement that BeAnn typed for Judy and Martina in 1986 came to the forefront.

Given the state of mind of all three when they met at Wimbledon, there is every reason to believe that each one's memory was fuzzy. If BeAnn misrepresented herself (as a lawyer), then Martina would not have to honor the contract entered into with Judy. If BeAnn was misrepresenting herself (as a lawyer), then Martina was operating under an entirely different set of assumptions when she signed the cohabitation agreement. If BeAnn was misrepresenting herself, Martina stood to protect half of her acquired assets. By the time this matter came before a court of law in 1991, all parties had valid reasons for their separate interpretations. Martina's defense suggests that BeAnn was covering up her employer's alleged role in the perpetration of the document, while Judy's memory serves to support her belief that Martina was a willing and active participant in the design and implementation of the document. This issue is still unresolved and is the subject of future litigation.

"Martina looked up at me in the box seats reserved for only the players' families and guests. It was a look in her eyes and a slight upward tilt of the head that I would see over and over again after each of her victories over the next seven years. Sometimes I could see the tears of joy glistening from far away. And sometimes there was a spontaneous wink that let us know she was happy about winning, but more happy about being with me. I was always proud. And then there was always our special and secret sign of holding the last two fingers on our hands together, leaving three fingers up, a sign that meant 'I love you.' It was our way of continually confirming our commitment and adoration for one another. That alone may be my dearest memory."

On Saturday afternoon, July 7, on center court, Chris and Martina played for the Wimbledon Championship title. Martina won in two sets, 7–6, 6–2. Martina had beaten Chris for the twelfth straight time and captured her fifth Wimbledon Championship title.

4

The Brisbane Ceremony

It was sunny and warm in Brisbane, Australia, in November 1984. It was summer in Brisbane, an enchanting city with miles of sandy beaches. Judy and Martina had traveled nearly twenty hours by air to get there. It was time for Martina to play another Virginia Slims tournament. She used this tournament as a warm-up on the grass surfaces before playing the grass court Grand Slam Tournament—the Australian Open. But this year would be different from all the rest—the tournament would be a secondary focus. On November 17, 1984, in Brisbane, Australia, Martina and Judy planned to consummate their relationship by making a commitment for life—by pledging their lives to each other in the sight of God, "until death did them part." They had been together constantly for nearly eight months. Judy re-counted, "After many private talks about lifestyle and philosophies and families and love, we were ready to celebrate and confirm our relationship in a most traditional way. We were going to exchange our vows in a church. This way was the only way I knew, and Martina seemed comfortable with the choice. Not being sure how two women go about this, as usual I asked Martina."

The day they arrived at their hotel, the Sheraton, they headed out on foot to find a church where they could later exchange vows, privately, without a minister or even a friendly witness. They didn't have to search far. They found a small, traditional church perched on a hill just a block from their hotel. The angular cathedral building had high-reaching steeples and beautiful stained-glass windows that reached to the top of the roof. More importantly, it happened to be a John Wesley Mission Church, a bit of fate, Judy recalls thinking. "John Wesley founded the Methodist church, and I was a Methodist. I took this as a good sign, that things were falling into place."

Judy and Martina had purchased rings in New York and brought them to Brisbane. Judy had chosen for Martina a beautiful yellow-diamond ring which was mounted between two rows of diamond baguettes. For Judy, Martina had chosen a pale ruby ring called a "ruby light," which was cut in a rectangular shape, with tapering diamond baguettes on either side of the ruby.

Friday evening, after the day's tennis, the night before the ceremony, Judy and Martina decided to unwrap their rings, which had both been wrapped in tissue paper and hidden in their respective carry-on bags. Although they had shopped for rings together, they would now surprise each other with the rings they had actually selected.

Judy panicked. She couldn't find the ring she had bought for Martina. Somehow it had vanished since their arrival in Brisbane. "We looked everywhere for that ring," Judy recalls. "We called hotel security, we went through the trash cans, we questioned the maids, checked with room service, everything. Whether it was stolen out of the room or mistakenly thrown in the trash because it was in some tissue paper, we'll never know. We could never find that ring. Martina never placed it on her hand, which was heartbreaking for me because it was a really unusual diamond, and I knew she loved it as soon as she saw it in New York."

As always, Martina was emotionally generous and understanding, insisting that she didn't need a ring and that she was more than happy to go without one. The ceremony is what counted. Yet Judy knew she wanted to find a ring, if only for her own peace of mind. "I wanted to exchange something to complete the ritual." So she quietly slipped down to the hotel gift shop, the only place open at that time of night. She walked up to a display case that had various key chains dangling from multiple plastic arms. She spun the display rack around and one trinket caught

Judy, age two.

The young Hill family: brother
Sarge, father Sargent, mother
Frances, baby sister Jan, daughter
Judy (age five).

Judy as "Maid of Cotton" in 1965--
modeling in Paris with French model.

Judy leading thoroughbreds onto the racetrack as one of her official duties as "Maid of Cotton"—labeled "The Yellow Rose of Texas."

Dr. Ed Nelson.

December 16, 1967—Judy marries Edward R. Nelson, Jr.

Judy and Ed's sons in 1976: Bales, age three; Eddie, age five.

A ski trip in 1981: Ed, Judy, and Bales.

The first time together: Martina and Judy with Judy's nephew and sons in 1984.

Self photo: Judy and Martina in Paris in 1984 during the French Open, when Martina won the Grand Slam in tennis.

A casual evening at home in Fort Worth in 1985: Martina, Judy, and Bales.

A family diving trip to the St. James Club in Antigua in 1987: Eddie, Bales, Judy, diving instructor Burt Kerschner, and Martina.

Judy with Martina's family in Germany: Martina, Judy, sister Jana, father Mirek, and mother Jana.

Judy's parents, Sarge and Frances Hill, at a Thanksgiving dinner while in Australia for the Australian Open in 1985.

A "Czech roast sausage" in Puerto Rico in 1985: Judy and Martina.

On top of Aspen Mountain on Christmas Eve, 1986: Ron Chauner, Judy, Santa, and Martina.

Self photo: Judy and Martina, December 1986.

Martina and friends in Aspen, 1986: BeAnn Sisemore, Martina, and interior designer Jaye Skaggs.

Martina, Don Johnson, and Judy in Miami, 1987.

Wimbledon, 1987: Dr. Renee Richards, Judy, Martina, Sugar Ray Leonard, and Aja Zanova.

Having fun at a pro-celebrity tournament in Aspen: Jan Newman, Svatka Hoshel, Judy, and Martina.

Judy at a 1985 pro-celebrity tournament in Atlantic City.

Coaches and family on tour: trainer Joe Breedlove, Jana, Judy, coach Randy Crawford, and Mirek Navratil.

her eye: a brightly colored key chain, from which dangled a replica of Australia. She quickly slipped it off the rack and onto her finger. Judging by how large it was for her, she sensed that it might fit Martina perfectly. She purchased the key ring and tossed the continental miniature in the trash, as her mind wandered to a movie scene where the lead characters were too poor to afford a real wedding ring. She thought romantically, "If the Unsinkable Molly Brown could settle for a cigar band, surely Martina and I can settle for a wire key ring." Judy kept the key ring a secret, hidden from Martina's view, wanting to surprise her at the ceremony.

The couple got up early in the morning, dressed nervously for the occasion in informal clothes. They dressed for each other, free to please themselves, for this was not a bride-and-groom wedding, and they felt no need to imitate the black-and-white figures found perched atop a four-tier white cake. They then headed out in the quiet of the morning and walked to the church.

Judy remembers the morning well: "I remember it was a beautiful day. There was a sense of excitement that could be felt by both of us. This was an emotional day for me, one filled with unrelated dreams and expectations. I was very nervous. Even though we had been together since March, and we had often talked about this, did we really want to proceed? Did we want to consummate the fact that we wanted to make a commitment for life? I was making a commitment to live with another woman for the rest of my life. That's a really big step. It was different from my marriage to Ed. I was much older now, and I was not only committing myself to Martina, I was committing myself to a new way of life. I also had two children to consider.

"When we reached the church, we were happy to see that the doors were open and no one was around. The church looked inviting, and our fears about being locked out were quickly eliminated. The possibility that we might be all dressed up and have nowhere to go had vanished. We had tried to eliminate this problem prior to the moment, but we could think of no subtle way of casually inquiring about the church's public accessibility without drawing undesired attention to ourselves. Even in Brisbane, the paparazzi were still a privacy threat. So, without any viable solution, we simply trusted that we would be able to enter the church without delay. Everything was going as planned."

They each breathed a sigh of relief as they walked through the massive doors of the brick church. Then they gently smiled at each other, acknowledging to themselves, in a code shared only by the closest of friends, that they were pleased to be alone and ready to begin. They walked down the aisle, relieved to see that there was no one in the church, and proceeded directly to the altar. Facing each other, they prepared to make their respective commitments. Each had carefully chosen her own words that would express an emotional commitment to her love. They had spent time thinking about what they wanted to express, but up until that moment neither person knew what the other was going to say. The promises were quite traditional—lacking only the presence and words of a minister—but they each vowed to be faithful for the rest of their lives, till death did them part. "I even remember being touched that Martina had made what I thought was a special effort to make me feel comfortable, for the commitment vows we made would have been much the same for a heterosexual couple."

Martina went first, and after she had made her vows, she slipped the ruby ring onto Judy's finger. Judy then spoke promises to Martina, after which she proudly pulled out the key ring and slipped it on Martina's left ring finger. "Tears welled up in both our eyes as we instantly recognized the sentiment behind the symbol."

Judy remembers thinking that there was something romantic about the copper ring, a nonmaterialistic and sentimental trinket with great personal significance. "The ring fit her finger perfectly, and she actually wore it for several months, even though the copper kept turning her finger green. We always laughed about it. She never took it off until we replaced it with a thin gold band that was small enough to leave on her hand when she held a racket. I wore one just like it beneath my ruby and diamond ring (one which I never took off until several months after Martina told me that she no longer wore hers—that was in February of 1991). In 1985 I had a gold replica made of the copper ring. I gave it to her in Venice."

With the words spoken and the promises made, Judy and Martina walked back up the aisle. Just as they opened the doors to go outside, the church bells began to chime, as if on cue. They stopped to listen to the bells and felt at peace with themselves. Judy recalls, "It was as though God or someone was saying, 'This is okay—this is good.' It was like being blessed somehow, some divine approval that it was right, it was a good and happy thing." Commitment is its own reward.

That afternoon, Martina practiced while Judy went shopping for a sunset picnic on the beach. For the occasion, Judy had brought with her from Texas a striped brown beach towel on which in black script were the words "Martina and Judy, 11–17–84." They eventually framed the towel and hung it on various walls in their houses throughout their relationship. Guests must have been curious about its significance, but no one was ever bold enough to ask.

The ceremony in Brisbane was private, and Judy never told her friends or her family about it until after the breakup in 1991. She had known it as one of the happiest days of her life, yet it was something special between the two of them that she wanted to keep private in the midst of a highly public lifestyle, traveling the world with one of the sport's most popular stars. They were private people and they cherished their private moments, which were too few and far between.

When Judy eventually revealed the news of her marriage to her sons, Eddie (now twenty-two) and Bales (now nineteen), they both responded with astonishment. "Mom, you married Martina? Oh come on, Mom, you *married* her?" Judy had been living with Martina for seven years and the boys loved her; they thought of her as family. But they expressed the need to attach a label, or give her a role that would identify her place in their family. She was simply Martina, and they had grown to accept the relationship. The idea that their mother walked into a church and exchanged vows with the world's No. 1 female tennis player was something they never visualized as a possibility. It was, in their minds, something that would be reserved for a man and a woman—their mother and father. Well, maybe it was all right for some same-sex couples, but they still couldn't imagine it for their mother.

Yet after reflecting upon the news for an hour or so, Bales confessed to his mother, "You know, Mom, that was all right." He understood what the relationship had meant to his mother and why it would be important for his mother and Martina to pledge themselves to each other in that way.

5

Life Before Martina

Like most of us, Judy found herself on a journey that was both personal and political as she moved through particular stages of her adult life. She was faced with many of the same challenges shared by other female baby boomers as she struggled for her own identity during the sexual revolution, tried to please her husband during their marriage, and attempted to be a perfect mother to her sons, all the while trying to succeed at her own internal journey towards true self-esteem.

Judy Elaine Hill was born on September 17, 1945, in Fort Worth, Texas. She was the middle child of three, all raised in a religious home. Her brother Sargent was born in 1943 and her sister Jan in 1950.

Judy's parents, Sargent and Frances Hill (called Bigs and Ma by their children and grandchildren) had been born and raised in Fort Worth and were prominent members of the community, owning and operating several Bonanza Steak House restaurants and movie theaters and participating in charity events and social functions.

Sargent Hill is a handsome, well-educated man who earned his master's degree in business administration from Pepperdine University in Los Angeles. His father as a young man was both a Methodist circuit minister who rode his horse from church to church, delivering sermons, and a postman for the U.S. Post Office most of his life. Judy and her siblings were raised as Methodists.

Sargent is a man who finds comfort in rituals. For example, he and several of his friends meet every Saturday morning at the Carriage House in Fort Worth, with each man suggesting one of the dishes for breakfast. After sharing a meal and socializing, they head for the golf course. This group is the last of a dying breed: men of some wealth and local prestige who are the "good old boys" of Texas politics and tradition. Their circle is closed and tight, and obviously women and children are not invited. This circle of friends acts as a safe harbor for Sarge. He knows what to expect from them. While most of them might disapprove of Judy's lifestyle, they wouldn't disapprove openly of Judy. Thus, as awkward and public as the situation would become during Judy and Martina's hearing in September 1991, Sarge didn't skip his Saturday rendezvous. The hearing had made the front page of the Fort Worth newspaper all week, and again that morning, as Martina publicly accused the Hills and Nelsons of conspiring against her, but it was never discussed at the group's breakfast. Talking about it would shame Sarge's family. The other men could acknowledge his struggle with their eyes, but not with their words. This was an unspoken agreement among Texas gentlemen. We all seek shelter in our own private ways.

Sargent and Frances Hill have been married for over fifty years and, as of this day, no one has ever heard Frances swear. Very likely this reflects the influence of her rock-ribbed grandparents who had moved to Texas in a covered wagon in 1879. They had a family and worked the land. Frances's parents raised seven girls and five boys. Frances was the baby of the family.

Frances Hill is a beautiful, seventyish woman of average height, who passed on to Judy her light green eyes, fair skin, and well-proportioned features. She had done some modeling herself in Dallas, and was proud of her daughter's appearance, but she also did everything possible to assist Judy with her cultural and social development. This attention and experience enabled Judy to win her most prestigious beauty title, National Maid of Cotton, in 1965. Only nineteen, she was the youngest woman ever selected to become the cotton industry's "fashion ambassadress."

"It's not actually a beauty contest," Judy is quick to point out. "It's a contest to find the best young woman for the job—as a national spokesman for a major industry—and if she is nice looking that is a big plus. If it were just a beauty contest, they would call her the Queen of Cotton." Judy took her job seriously and enjoyed the responsibilities and duties associated with her title.

On the cover of the 1966 application pamphlet is a picture of Judy with President Lyndon Johnson at the White House. When asked about the picture, she said that she had written the President—who was from Texas—and told him she would be in town and would like to meet him. Cotton Council officials had no idea she would be so bold as to write like this, nor that her strategy would succeed.

Judy recalled, "It was very important for the cotton industry to keep their contacts in Washington for lobbying purposes. So, every year, they set up things for the Maid of Cotton to do while in Washington, D.C. Each year, for example, she attends a luncheon given by the industry. Jim Wright was my congressman, and he hosted the luncheon and sat next to me. On my other side was Tip O'Neill, the Speaker of the House. We started talking, and someone said, 'Gee, it would be great if you could meet with LBJ.' I told them that I had written a note to President Johnson, on my Maid of Cotton stationery, telling him I would like to meet him while in Washington, and a week later I got an emergency call from the Cotton Council, telling me that I had been invited to the White House. This would be the first time a president would meet with a Maid of Cotton."

The meeting went well. LBJ was curious to know how college students felt about the Vietnam War and particularly how Judy felt about it. He had two daughters close to her age, and he felt comfortable talking to her about how young people perceived the political world around them. They spent fifteen minutes alone in the Rose Garden (with only the Secret Service men present), and Judy proved to herself that, despite her age, she could meet anyone and remain poised and confident. Judy's journal entry on Friday, May 7, 1965, read:

TODAY I MET THE PRESIDENT OF THE UNITED STATES. It was the most exciting, wonderful, fabulous experience of my life. First I met the Secretary of Agriculture, Orville Freeman. Then I was taken to the White House to meet Lyndon B. Johnson. He was a majestic man. Looked very tired and like a man with much concern and a man who was concerned with the lives of all people. He talked, laughed, and looked at the Rose Garden outside his office. He called in the press and within seconds—hundreds of reporters—CBS, NBC, ABC, UPI—all were watching as we talked. Afterwards I went into the Press Room and was rushed by reporters as to what I had said and what he said to me. I then went to a luncheon—Mrs. Jim Wright was there and also the wife of the Secretary of Health, Education and Welfare.

The Maid of Cotton role was much more than a fleeting beauty-contest experience for Judy. She would return to college for her senior year, motivated to pursue a modeling and television career. The following year, and up to her thirty-fifth birthday, she worked as a model for Neiman-Marcus in Fort Worth and Dallas.

There are stereotypes about women who have been raised to become beauty contestants and fashion models. Some of these stereotypes are merely misogynistic, while others are valid because they are produced by unnatural lives, where appearances are central and anger is rarely voiced. When a teenage girl is trained to be judged by a panel of men on appearance and is expected to talk in loving and sweet tones about polite and charming issues, her genuine voice is muted and she is infantalized at best and dehumanized at worst. When beauty and charm are expected, it is difficult to be authentic, regardless of your own motives.

While Judy placed a great deal of value on her own wit and humor, others focused on her appearance. Her own self-image was affected by those around her. Therefore, it wasn't surprising when Judy one day commented that she felt Martina was with her because, as Martina said, "Judy turns heads when she walks into a room."

As Maid of Cotton, Judy wore cotton fashions and traveled

the world as an important spokesperson for the industry. To sell young women this dream in 1965, the Cotton Council put out literature that promised the winner "the experience of a lifetime." Under that heading they described her duties:

> Winning the Maid of Cotton selection is like having a dream come true. Suddenly you find yourself flying on a grand intercontinental tour dressed in clothes fit for a princess . . . being honored by famous people at banquets and balls in elegant places . . . lunching with movie stars . . . holding press conferences . . . chatting with ambassadors . . . posing for magazine covers . . . and smiling for television cameras. On you the spotlight shines for seven whirlwind months and, at the end of your fabulous odyssey, you drive home in a brand-new Ford with luggage packed with clothes created by the world's leading designers.

Balancing her beauty-queen veneer, Judy was blessed with a positive self-image, formed at an early age when she was given love and affection by her family. Unlike most beauty contestants, who tend to come from blue-collar families, Judy had an upper-middle-class upbringing. She was not pushed into parading down a ramp at an early age, singing and smiling her way into the hearts of local judges. She was given dance and music lessons, as were her siblings, but her looks did not command a lot of attention until high school. Rather than being cultivated to become a beauty queen, she merely fell into it because she became beautiful and sexy. As a participant, she was sponsored or nominated by people who approached her and encouraged her to participate or compete in these functions. This distinction is important because, while her parents never pushed her to find self-worth in the process, we as a society ask beautiful women to parade and smile for us; in return, we promise them large rewards for pleasing and indulging our desires.

When Judy entered Texas Christian University (she was voted "Howdy Week Queen" as a freshman), she decided to major in broadcast journalism and speech. This seemed like an obvious choice for a beauty queen who had become a skillful speaker, her voice deep and rich, well paced, with a deliberate cadence and a soft Texas drawl. However, during her senior year at TCU, she met and fell in love with Ed Nelson, a premedical student. Her dreams of television journalism suddenly competed with her desire to become a wife and a mother.

Judy had just returned from her one year "reign" as Maid of Cotton to finish her junior year. Upon her return, she was made the pledge trainer for her sorority, and this ultimately led her to Ed Nelson. Her recollection:

"As the pledge director, I had to attend all the pledge parties. My pledges were going to have a party with the Delts, our brother fraternity, and one of my sorority sisters asked me if I would go to the party with the president of the Delts. I said 'No, I don't go on blind dates.' She insisted that I would like him, declaring, 'He's a really neat guy, vice president of the student body, and handsome.' I promised to check him out at the party. He showed up with one of my sorority sisters, and I could see what I was missing. Later, he brought his date back to the sorority house, and I happened to be standing in the hall. I watched him kiss her good night and I felt really jealous, but I didn't even know this guy. So I went back to the sorority sister who had originally asked me to go out with Ed and told her I had seen him and I changed my mind. If she wanted to give him my phone number, that would be fine with me. He called in a couple of days and asked me to go with him to a football game. So we started dating in September, got engaged in December, and we were married a year later."

Prior to meeting Martina, Judy had never had any inkling of homosexual tendencies. She had a boyfriend, "Rocky," from first until fourth grade. They shared their first kiss one spring afternoon while in the third grade. "It was just a little kiss," Judy recalls, "but we talked about it, discussed it, and actually planned it for a long time." Her first real boyfriend was "a guy named Kurt." He was in the eighth grade and Judy was in the ninth, and their relationship continued "on and off" until she was a sophomore in college. Once she was at TCU, she says, "I dated *all* the time."

After Judy married Ed, she had to find a way to support them while he completed medical school. Her father had been an executive with Bonanza Steak House, though not involved with the franchising side, but the Hills were obviously familiar with the business. Judy recalls, "I was a pioneer of sorts. My mother and a friend of hers from Houston put up the money for me to buy a Bonanza franchise near TCU. I ran it, managed it, did everything. I paid back their investment within a year, made a salary, and even had a profit. I was in the clear."

Judy's first son, Eddie, was born in March 1971. When she worked at Bonanza, she placed him in a playpen in her office. The business was successful, close to the university, and was well staffed with sorority sisters. Judy and her father still disagree as to who actually counted the steaks each night. Sarge swears that Judy went home to care for her family while he stayed to do the counting. Judy remembers staying there after closing, allowing the students to go home and study, while she counted the steaks. Whatever the truth may be, Judy's restaurant sold enough steaks to consistently rank among the top ten in sales throughout the chain.

By the time Bales was born in October 1973, the Nelsons' marriage was slowly deteriorating, but Judy was unaware. Three years later they separated, with Judy keeping the boys and staying in the house. Ed was going through many changes in his own life and wanted to be on his own for a while. During this trial separation, which lasted two years, Judy spent most of the time with the boys and delighted in them; they were the joy of her life.

When Judy and Ed reconciled, they tried hard to make the marriage work. But the damage was irreparable. Judy tried her utmost to become the perfect doctor's wife, but the more she assumed the role of the "total woman," the more angry and upset she became. While Ed had decided to settle down on this second go-around, Judy was becoming increasingly discontented with the marriage. The "total woman" image just didn't seem to fit her idea of being herself.

Those close to the couple viewed Judy as stable and strong

through this rough period, and they treated her with kindness and respect. Yet some of those same people were harshly judgmental of Judy when eventually she left Ed and joined Martina. They failed to understand that Ed's behavior hadn't changed much during the second part of the marriage. Instead, Judy had to adjust her behavior to satisfy his needs and keep the family together. While those friends could understand Judy's unhappiness with her marriage, they could not understand and support her own need for growth and happiness outside the marriage. It was somehow fine for Ed to "sow his wild oats," but if Judy wanted support from these same people for her gay lifestyle, she was simply living in a tree.

Several months before Judy met Martina, she sent a desperate message to Ed at his office. She placed the note inside a greeting card, telling him that she was lonely and felt she was no longer in love with him, and she was scared. Having no response from Ed, Judy several days later asked him at home, "Did you get my card?"

"Yes, I read it," he replied, "but I got busy with a patient and forgot all about it." He never mentioned it to her again. At that moment Judy knew that her marriage was really over.

This is not meant to suggest that Judy turned to Martina as a reaction to a failing marriage. That judgment is far too simplistic, and sexuality is far more complex and multidimensional than this. The question raised is "Could it have been any woman other than Martina?"

To begin to construct an answer to this question, we first need to establish Judy's ideas about relationships in general. Judy does not stratify relationships and love. She acknowledges the differences, but she does not see nonsexual relationships as extremely different from sexual ones. She is capable of loving her children, her friends, her family, her horses, the mountains, with incredible intensity.

Judy tends to formalize her connections by forming business relationships with family and friends. She had been in business with her parents and husband in the past, and she had hired friends to work in her restaurant. It was therefore not out of place for her to form a business relationship with Martina—she does business with the people in her family, and she is close to the people with whom she does business.

An interesting aspect about Judy's approach to connections is that by deemphasizing what is sexual, she eliminates the need to struggle with the political or social implications of her relationships. While others label Judy's relationships, she is content to neutralize their comments with gender-neutral labels like "companion" and "friend." Judy believes that the labels "heterosexual," "homosexual," and "bisexual" need to be deemphasized and that the word sexual can stand alone. As many have said, the prefixes "homo," "bi," and "hetero" are classic examples of the adjective being the enemy of the noun. Sexuality is an extension of friendship, a continuum, a special and tender cement between two people.

While these beliefs are sensitive and admirable, it seems obvious that these definitions and classifications serve as a protective barrier, shielding Judy and her family from insensitive and unkind remarks made by others. This "romantic friendship" angle seems to reconcile her Methodist upbringing and her political reality. Without dwelling on motives, Judy has found a framework that she is comfortable with, a way of talking that emphasizes the personal and emotional, while playing down the political or sexual.

Judy feels that the label "lesbian" has a very negative connotation. She said, "I feel we all use labels too carelessly and usually in context that disassociates reality from anything positive or constructive." Judy sees herself as an activist in her battle to have the state of Texas recognize her right to enter into any business contract, regardless of her sexual preference.

Martina was not simply another woman. She was *Martina*, a household name, a multimillionaire, the number-one tennis player in the world. Martina could give Judy something which every parent wants for their children: resources and opportunity.

Yet, despite all the privileges that Eddie and Bales would gain from their mother's relationship with Martina, they would be

separated from her for days at a time while she traveled on tour
during the next seven years. Judy toured with Martina for all but
several weeks each year, and though Martina had the means to
have the children join them whenever they wanted to see their
mother, they were still in school and spent most of their time
with their father and grandparents while Judy traveled.

"They never had to ask us if they could come," Judy assents.
"They just called and told us that they wanted to come, and we
simply arranged for a ticket. This was my deal; they could visit
me whenever they wanted to—this would never change." Not a
day went by that Judy didn't communicate with her sons.

Martina could provide a buffer to Judy's guilt by allowing the
boys a glamorous life, first-class travel, no questions asked. This
meant that planes were chartered to fly them from Fort Worth
to Aspen on Christmas Day, or that they would join Martina and
Judy for the holidays and the skiing that they all loved and
shared. It was always a special family time. These teenage boys
had an amazing amount of power at an early age, but they had
been taught to be caring and loving, and those qualities were
always evident.

Judy recalls, "The times that were the most special to us as a
family unit were spent in Antigua. It was there that the four of us
(and in later years our two "adopted sons" who were the best
friends of Eddie and Bales) would spend private and happy moments away from the cameras and the attention of the public and
their perceptions of this unusual family structure. We shared
jokes and ran on the beach. We cooked out on our own patio and
watched the sunset. We made home videos that will remain
classics forever—Bales being the director and Eddie usually the
star! Of course, we *all* had our cameos—our moments on the
screen—unretouched and unrehearsed. We were all 'hams.'
Those videos are priceless memories of our days as a happy and
almost normal family. In our eyes, we were *all* always normal.
The energy of a happy family is the same, be it heterosexual or
same sex. How can we dare to make true happiness and honesty
otherwise?"

She continued, "Antigua became our special 'second home.'

The boys and I would play tennis with Martina, and the kid in her prevailed—she was as relaxed and happy at these moments as I had ever seen her. It was that childlike quality about her that I loved so much. We even all learned to scuba dive there; we took a course and were certified. Our diving instructor, Bert Kerschner, and his wife, Faye, and their children would become some of our best friends. Burt and Faye made Martina and me the 'godmothers' of their son. What a joy. We were truly breaking through barriers of prejudices. It felt good. I was proud. I think Martina was, too."

Unlike others who may argue that homosexuality is biologically based, Judy felt she was not compelled to be with women, but was merely drawn to Martina. Any oppression Judy might experience would be from an outgrowth of her personal choice rather than one imposed upon her by lack of options. Perhaps it could have been someone other than Martina. Someone extraordinary, someone compelling.

Change rarely happens in an instant; it is a long, cumulative process which has far-reaching roots. Judy's conversion experience had its seeds at an early age, when she became aware that girls and boys experienced the world differently, and that Southern girls have deeply ingrained ideas about themselves in relationship to others. She describes the process in her own words:

"In retrospect, the issue of my sexuality—of how I came to make the choice that I have made in my life—is not about loving a woman, it is about *being* a woman.

"In order to make this statement, I know that I must answer some questions. I want to go back in my life and explore the events and concepts that molded my behavior, my ideas and ideals—to explore the choices that, at last, made me free to be the person that was struggling to be authentic. I always knew that I had to be true to myself. Expressing that truth took years. And I know that today, in spite of my Southern upbringing and 'total woman' aspirations, I do, at times, experience that authenticity. And what an exhilarating feeling that is. I laugh. I really laugh.

"As a child I was taught (perhaps as early as three or four) that a pretty little girl would grow up to marry a young man (someone handsome and kind, of course) and have children with him. We would live happily ever after. We (my husband and I) would, of course, be monogamous. Had I been interested only in women at an early age, I still would have wanted children. I know it was something that I was *taught* to want, but having children was, more importantly, something that I genuinely wanted, and that feeling was separate and apart from everything I learned.

"Being pretty, or handsome, or at least always aspiring to be, was important in my family. My parents spoke to us in terms of good grooming, neatness; a certain caring about one's appearance. However, one's intellect and athletic ability were emphasized as part of the total picture. One's spiritualness was as essential to this vision of beauty as breathing—I was supposed to grow up to become a good and wholesome and beautiful person with never a sharp word for anyone.

"I never thought of myself as beautiful. I do know there is something about me, a certain aura, perhaps, that causes people to turn and look back. However, there was an embarrassing moment in my early childhood (it was the fifth grade, to be exact) when I was singled out by my schoolteacher, Mrs. Forrester, and scolded in front of my classmates for being the only girl in class whom all the boys wanted for their girlfriend. She told the boys that there were enough girls in the class for each one of them to have a separate girlfriend. I wanted to crawl in a hole and hide. Why had she done this to me in front of my peers? At this point, my girlfriends became angry and jealous. Until my teacher pointed out the dilemma, I wasn't aware there was a problem. But I knew from that day on that things were different for me and that, for whatever reason, I was often looked at and sought after in such a way that put me on the defensive and made me uncomfortable.

"The older I got, the more apparent this became—men would always look, many would make sexual advances—I stopped them in their tracks. You could look but *not* touch. Mother taught me that. That was a lesson that most mothers taught their daughters. It was the creed of the 'good girls.' I learned my lessons well. I was prepared to be the good girl that my parents had taught me to be. All of my life, at least until I broke out of that mold when I went with Martina, I tried to be the perfect role model—be it daughter, student, wife, or mother.

"Inside I burned with rage. I became so tired of always being focused upon as an object rather than a person. I was always on guard—always polite and gracious and charming, but never letting any man too close. I was uncomfortable, to say the least, but I never openly expressed this anger. Even after I was married, my husband's friends would 'come on' to me—their wives were often my close friends. When I would find the courage to speak to my husband about this, he would say that I should take it as a compliment and that it's just the way guys were. I didn't like it. I still don't.

"From the day I realized that there was a 'double standard' sexually (I was probably twelve at the time), I was furious. I told my mother that it just wasn't fair—I didn't understand why boys could be sexually permissive and be thought of as 'cool' and girls (of my generation) who let boys go too far were regarded as bad, as sluts. I certainly was never willing to lower my high *standards*, but instead I demanded that the rules be equal between the boys and the girls. They were not. But, like the good girl I was expected to be, I, too, let that pass. Deep down inside of me, this imbalance of power just didn't seem right—we were all human beings, and the rules by which we lived should not be different, nor separated by gender.

"Indeed, as I grew older, the fact that I, as were so many women were treated first as sex objects, and only later for other abilities and talents. It was bewildering. I didn't know how to change this—I didn't see that I ever could. I learned to live with it, to accept it. I compromised in my outlook because society dictated that I do so. On the outside I appeared happy, but inside I was miserable.

"As I grew older, monogamy became increasingly important. It still is. I was taught as a teenager that seeking a monogamous relationship when I married was critical to the survival of that union. I did not question this either. It seemed to fall right in line with everything else I had been taught. I certainly expected it of myself and of my partner. I refused to question the consequences of what would happen to the relationship if either of us veered from that standard. I later had to face that very problem in my marriage when my husband played around. I was not prepared to deal with it. I was taught that a good and happy marriage combined with open communication would breed only monogamy (no pun intended). I was taught that surely if I was the 'total' woman—beautiful, giving, bright, the perfect housewife and lover and mother—I could not fail; that goodness begets goodness. What a myth!

"It's no wonder to me now that at some point in my life I would rebel against these principles which proved invalid. It's no surprise to me now that finally I released some of that anger and rid myself of some of the fears by turning to a woman for love and companionship and equality. It's no surprise that at this point in my life I may still choose to do so. It is no surprise that I was totally relaxed with Martina, whereas I would never have allowed myself to have that 'lunch' with a man. It's no surprise that at long last, I found myself able to share my ideals and philosophies on an equal basis without any fear—with no guard up—for this was a woman, someone who shared many of the same feelings and dealt with the same issues. It all computed. It worked. There was no fear that I would damage a man's ego and that he would reject me. I could, at last, be equal. I was a person in my own right, not just a sexual object. In the beginning this is how I saw it. It felt good. It was comfortable. In retrospect, perhaps it was naïve of me to think all would be different simply because I chose to be with a woman. But in so many ways it was better because being female in our society still does not allow you the privileges enjoyed by a man. So, at least, by *living* with a woman, I no longer had to compromise myself. I can be authentic. I am not merely an object. I can work, be creative, make money, and be successful without threatening the male ego.

"For all of the years before meeting Martina, I managed as well as anyone to become what our culture thinks of as an ideal American woman. Why not? My mother was the perfect role model. She was, herself, very beautiful. Her looks are important to her. She has wonderful eyes and a Southern kind of innocence about her that always attracted men. Good grooming, just the right dress, shoes, and accessories were essential to her. Her taste was impeccable. She passed her standards on to me and to my sister. I was taught that my appearance was just as necessary as good grades in school or what office I might have held on the student council. It was all part of the package: to be the best I could be. And to my parents' credit, I was also taught that how I was on the inside was just as important as what people saw on the outside. What I found was that I was never given the chance for people to see what was on the inside—they never got past how I looked.

"My father, dashingly handsome, was able to reassure me about my beauty and charm relative to men's observations. He also took the time to develop my athletic talents which mother lacked but which added to my appeal—the 'total package.' The few times I veered from the 'total woman' (and I did . . . mostly when I was a child, trying to find the boundaries of this perfect image) such as wearing jeans, climbing trees, going barefoot, and playing cowboys with the boys instead of dolls with the girls, I was reminded that this was not the image planned for Judy Elaine Hill. A pretty little girl should wear a dress, play with dolls, and take voice lessons, especially if she wanted to grow up to be Miss America (which is something that almost every Southern mother wishes for her daughter, and mine was no exception).

"Obviously, I grew up in a protected environment. I grew up in a part of the country and from a generation where the women (of our class) never worked outside of the home. All the women that I knew (my mother and her friends) were housewives. That is not to say that they didn't work—they worked harder than the men. Their jobs were endless and multifaceted. The hours worked were more like eighteen rather than the customary eight in the workplace. But still, the women were not 'professionals'— they were, in every sense of the word, 'the woman *behind* the man.' This did not seem right to me either. So, like every other feeling that I had that was different from what I was taught, I merely locked it up inside myself.

"Most girls from my generation and within my social structure were taught from a very early age that what we, as women, *must* aspire to be were good wives and mothers—to 'stand behind our man . . . to make him proud.' Our objective was to produce beautiful, bright children with high morals and good manners. We were to keep our men satisfied in bed. We were taught that going to college was important only in order to have a degree as some sort of insurance policy in case anything were to happen to our husbands (certainly not divorce), for, generally speaking, the women tended to outlive the men. At which time, if you were not prepared for his untimely death, you might have to get a job to support yourself. (We were never told who would take care of the house and the kids if this should ever happen.)

"On the surface, this philosophy and structure worked. I was bright, pretty to most, athletic, and energetic. I knew just how to get a man's attention, and I had learned how to hold him at bay. I was, above all, a *good* girl and aimed at becoming a perfect wife. Now, that sounds great, but what was going on inside was a different matter. Inside was a girl, a woman who wanted to be herself. She wanted to say what she believed in. She wanted to certainly be thought of as anyone's equal (or at least have to right to be). She wanted to be political, to disagree with the norm if she didn't think it was right or fitting. She wanted a voice. And she didn't want to seem threatening but instead to be accepted— not because she was a woman, but because she was a human being.

"After thirty-eight years, this voice inside me had to be heard. My friends would listen, but they, too, were often as stifled and inhibited as I was—therefore nothing changed, nothing was accomplished. The boys, the men in our lives were and always would be the voices, the decision makers. And why? Because our society gave them permission. It was given to them from the day they were born. The women of my generation had to change the rules for themselves in order to be granted the equality they so badly wanted. For me, this change began with my choice to go with Martina. Then I, in essence, risked everything I had and loved and held dear. To be true to myself. 'I will be me. I will be authentic.' And even though the relationship with Martina did not last a lifetime, it was worth the risk. I was changed forever; at last I was myself, the person I always knew I was and could be.

"If there is anything of value that I have learned from having taken the risks and having made the choices that I have made, it is that there is nothing better in the world than being yourself. There is no one way, no right way to live. Just be true to yourself, take care of yourself, and *that* is the very best person that you can give to the world. There is no 'set pattern,' there is no 'perfect image.' We are individuals, and each of us has something to contribute—give to yourself, be kind to yourself, laugh at yourself and with yourself—then, I promise, you will be giving a gift to everyone around you. The courage that you need you already have—it's there inside you."

6

Martina:
Life Before Judy

Martina Subertova was born to Jana and Mirslov Subert on October 18, 1956, in Prague, Czechoslovakia. Her name derives from a ski lodge in the Czechoslovakia mountain range of Kirkonose, where both parents had been ski instructors and where she was conceived. The lodge was called "Martinova," which loosely translated means "Martin's place."

Martina's mother returned to the Kirkonose Mountains, rejoining Martina's father, shortly after Martina was born. It was here that Martina, at the age of three, learned to ski. A year later, when Jana and Mirslov's marriage dissolved, Jana returned to her mother's hometown of Revnice, just outside of Prague. This was the town Martina called home for fifteen years.

Martina's father continued to live in Prague for four years before committing suicide when Martina was eight. She had visited him occasionally in Prague during those years before his death, but he was emotionally unstable and had little interest in her. Martina was told only that her father died during an operation to repair a stomach problem, and it wasn't until she was twenty-three that she learned the truth. She was informed of his suicide by her mother and stepfather, during their visit to the United States while she was living with Rita Mae Brown in Virginia, according to her autobiography *Martina*. A family conversation about Martina's lifestyle turned explosive, and her family hostilely informed her that she was much like her suicidal father, who suffered from extreme behavioral highs and lows. They warned her that she could ultimately share his unfortunate fate.

Martina's mother had married Mirek Navratil, her second husband, in 1961, whereupon her life reportedly improved immediately. By all reports, Mr. and Mrs. Navratil were a contented couple, providing their children with affection and attention at home. They all moved into an upstairs room in her mother's parents' house, sharing the same floor with her grandparents. The family soon grew to include a sister, Jana, born on June 20, 1963. Martina grew close to her maternal grandmother, but by her own admission, considered her grandfather a grump. He had divorced her grandmother but continued living in the same house. He grew increasingly eccentric and eventually became obsessed with keys and locks, locking family members out of the house when they were out in the yard for even a short time. Both Jana and Martina complained to their grandmother about their grandfather's behavior, placing her in the middle of their arguments.

Martina's paternal grandmother, Andela Subertova, eventually became Martina's emotional anchor. It was her grandmother's approving voice and soft image that carried Martina through her most ambitious emotional decision when, in 1975, she defected to the United States. Even as an adult, Martina remained her grandmother's "golden little girl" or "Holcicka," according to her friends. Martina was crushed to learn, in 1980, that Andela had died of cancer. After receiving a black-bordered funeral announcement, an emotionally devastated Martina phoned Prague and asked bewilderedly why no one had informed her that her grandmother had been ill. There was a striking similarity between her grandmother's passing and her father's passing. Each time Martina was given little information, and then only after the fact.

Fortunately, Mirek Navratil was an active man who enjoyed spending time outdoors with Martina, taking her mushroom hunting, to tennis courts, skiing. However, it was Martina's mother, Jana, who first put a tennis racket in Martina's hands at about age three. It was a full-size wooden racket once owned by her grandmother. As a result, Martina first learned to hit a two-handed backhand (which seems nearly inconceivable today, since Martina's trademark is a backhand slice, followed by a charge to the net). Jana had been an outstanding player herself, and she not only taught Martina the crucial basic skills at an early age, but instilled in her an enduring love for the game. Martina practiced for hours against backboards and fences. Destiny chose her to become one of the most gifted players ever to hold a racket.

While the standard of living was certainly lower in Czechoslovakia than in the United States, the quality of life was superior for Martina and her family. They never owned a car and didn't have hot running water until she was nearly grown, but they were able to take vacations each year and had access to great skiing and plenty of time for tennis. Thus Martina's athletic aspirations were encouraged by her family environment as well as her culture.

Prague has often been called the "Paris of the Eastern Bloc," given its stunning architecture and romantic setting. Yet, despite the beauty of its capital, Czechoslovakia has a history scarred by constant political turmoil. Martina was certainly aware of this turmoil and was affected personally by the tragic financial consequences her grandparents suffered after World War II, when Czechoslovakia became a communist state. In her autobiography, *Martina*, she points out that her family's thirty acres of fruit orchards, were expropriated by the government, and the family was left with only their cement house, a clay tennis court, and a relatively small piece of land. They had been stripped of the bountiful orchards which they could see from their windows, a constant reminder of the political and spiritual acquisition by a powerful and oppressive force.

The free-spirited Martina knew at an early age that she was better suited for democracy. As Skip Bayless reported in *Sports Illustrated*, "When Martina was in grade school, she pointed to a geography-book picture of the Empire State Building and told other Czech kids, 'I'm going to live there.' " Later in the article, Martina was quoted as saying, "I saw my country lose its nerve, lose its productivity, lose its soul. For someone with skill, a career, an aspiration, there was only one thing to do. Get out."

After the Communists took over in 1948, the National Tennis Association program was all but shut down. The late tennis expert Ted Tingling identified the salient reason that Martina was eventually forced to defect in 1975: "If you don't have people to feed back spontaneity, you don't get anyplace. It's such a quick exchange game. The heart of the matter is that tennis is so individual and Communist philosophy was afraid of developing individuality. That's the key to it all. You have to become an individual if you want to play tennis."

As Martina developed into a world-class player and traveled outside Czechoslovakia, her envy of the freedom enjoyed by other players was well documented. She loved the choices available to American women, who were free to come and go as they pleased, eat what they wanted, and travel as they pleased. During a tour in the United States in 1972—at sixteen—she took to capitalism like a duck to water, and it affected her body. She ate exactly what she wanted, including far too many hamburgers, and gained twenty pounds in a relatively short time.

Apparently, Martina's genuine appetite was for knowledge and like-minded friends, and as a result she chose political paths not available under Czech communism. During the U.S. Open in 1975, Martina defected to the United States. She had contemplated defection for a solid year, but needed time to sort out her emotions. The fact that she was now earning substantial money as a player influenced her decision. After winning $3,000 at the U.S. Open in 1974, she learned that the Czech government wanted it all—in cash. The American dollar, a hard currency, was greatly valued in Czechoslovakia, and the government capitalized on the opportunity to seize it from Czech players when they returned home. Martina had watched American players like Chris Evert spend their money freely. She could no longer ignore this contrast and embarked on her journey to become an American citizen.

Still, the decision to leave home in August 1975 was difficult. It was so wrenching emotionally, in fact, that she was unable to say goodbye to her grandmother or to anyone else. She simply packed her bags for the tour and never returned, believing she would never see her family again. According to close friends, Martina walled off her feelings, steeling herself from the pain and loss. Consequently, by necessity—rather than by choice or design—goodbyes have always been truncated and rapid for Martina. But, once committed to a choice, she makes the break and doesn't look back.

Once in the United States, Martina quickly surrounded herself with strong female friends, many of whom were feminists. She became close friends with the novelist Rita Mae Brown and tennis stars Rosie Casals and Billie Jean King. King and Casals, along with Martina, became movers and shakers in the Women's Tennis Association, demanding equal pay for female players in Grand Slam events. Yet, with her mind on so many new experiences and relationships, Martina was no longer focused solely on tennis. While her mind soared, her game suffered. She won only two tournaments in 1976, the year following her defection. But as the newness of her freedom wore off, she began to concentrate on her game and her fitness.

Running up to five miles a day and lifting weights on a rigorous program—in addition to her daily on-court practice sessions—Martina pushed herself to achieve a remarkable level of fitness. One of her lasting contributions to the game is that she forced women tennis players to become stronger and fitter in order to compete against her, and she inspired women in other sports to emulate her approach, which also included greater attention to better nutrition. Chris Evert even admitted, "Billie Jean King has made us into celebrities, but Martina has made us into athletes."

Though Martina defected in 1975, she would not become a naturalized citizen until 1981. For nearly six years, she lived with the fear that she would be denied citizenship, because she had become a controversial figure, always speaking her feminist mind. She took precautions not to travel over Communist countries while flying from one destination to the next, always asking for the air carrier's flight path and always avoiding the possibility that a flight might have to land due to mechanical problems.

Once in a Communist country, she feared she would be vulnerable without an American passport. However, that all ended when Martina, once and for all, became a U.S. citizen.

Chris Evert was Martina's greatest competitor. Starting in 1973 in Akron, Ohio, when Chris won their first match, 7–6, 6–3, and ending in 1989, when Chris retired from tennis, they competed in one of the greatest rivalries in sports history. Chris and Martina met seventy-eight times in match play.

Their styles both on and off the court were extremely different. Chris was perceived as the all-American girl who worked hard at her game. She was mentally tough, whereas Martina was always vulnerable to her own emotions and personal distractions.

It took Martina two years and six matches to finally win a match from Chris, in the quarterfinals in Washington: 3–6, 6–4, 7–6. Later that year (1975) at Forest Hills, during the U.S. Open, Chris played a grudge match, beating Martina in the semifinals 6–4, 6–4. At this point, she had beaten Martina twelve of the fourteen times they had met in tournament play. Not until 1976, in Houston, did Martina beat Chris in a tournament final, 6–3, 6–4.

While Chris was able to stay ahead of Martina for some time, she fell to Martina in three sets at Wimbledon in 1978, and admitted, "If Martina ever gets her head together, watch out." No sooner than Chris had uttered those words that Martina's hard work off the court coupled with renewed focus on the court began to pay off. Martina soared to number one for a short time, but was unable to remain focused. She had come to the United States without a coach and then spent years searching for the right person to work with her. She struggled to find a winning combination of player, coach, and trainer. Her coaches became frustrated by her emotional highs and lows, often forgetting that behind all the muscles and brains was a very young woman who needed and wanted to be loved and accepted in the United States.

Dr. Renee Richards, a practicing ophthalmologist and former tennis player, systematically rebuilt Martina's game after she was handed a humiliating loss by Chris Evert in 1981 at Amelia

Island, where she suffered a 6–0, 6–0 defeat. For nearly three years Dr. Richards worked with Martina on her strokes, tactics, and conditioning. However, Renee's sexuality had been a controversial point with many women tennis players for years. Renee had grown up as a man and then, at age forty, Richard Raskin underwent a sex change operation. After the operation she continued to compete, as a woman. While Richard was a good club-level player as a man, Renee sought a professional career as a female player. In 1976 she was banned from playing in the U.S. Open when she refused to take a chromosome test. One year later, after an appeal court reversed the decision, she competed in the 1977 U.S. Open. She reached as high as number fourteen in the world.

All of this added fuel to the fire already burning about Martina's lifestyle, and ludicrous rumors that Martina was also a former man began to circulate. No one, however, ever questioned the fact that Renee was an exceptional friend and coach to Martina, helping her win her first U.S. Open title in 1983.

Martina finally came up with the ideal team (for a while), when Nancy Lieberman joined her team, headed by coach Mike Estep. Nancy felt that Martina was too friendly with Chris Evert, on and off court, softening her competitive edge against a player who talked sweetly while she chewed you up and spit you out on court. Chris earned the label "Ice Princess" for good reason. She was all business on the court.

Lieberman pushed Martina to become physically and mentally fit, but by 1984, Martina had gotten as much out of Nancy as she could. She had become number one in the world with Nancy's guidance, and was able to retain her ranking, becoming more dominant each year. But perhaps Nancy had become overbearing, trying to turn Martina into a type of competitor that was counterintuitive to Martina. Suggestions made earlier by Lieberman, which once had been interpreted by Martina as productive, now seemed inappropriate. It was time to move on.

Martina held a record winning streak of seventy-three consecutive match wins, and stayed at number one for five consecutive years, before slipping to number two in the world, in 1987, after winning only four titles the entire year. Two of those titles, however, were Grand Slam tournament wins: the U.S. Open and Wimbledon. Martina was committed to becoming number one again, but Steffi Graff held tight to this position for three years.

In February 1989 Martina said, "I'm convinced I haven't played my best tennis yet. My technique is better than it's ever been. My coach [Craig Kardon] has worked on my serve, slowing me down. Before, I just walked up and hit the ball, which is silly. The serve is one part of the game you can control, so you shouldn't rush it." But Martina's serve wasn't the problem. It was her head. "I've been thinking too much," she admitted, "I might be thinking of three shots as the ball is coming to me. I'm too much a perfectionist. I've got to simplify my game and think just one shot, instead of deciding early where a shot should go, then changing my mind."

Martina's problem was not only that she thinks too much, but she reacts to distractions and criticism. She has faced humiliation when, as the number one or two player in the world, she was offered few product-endorsement contracts. Men yell insults at her from the stands, such as, "Martina is really a man." Money and friends can never truly shelter her from critics who find her aggressive style and muscular appearance offensive.

For years the public, naïve or biased, failed to appreciate Martina's open and honest manner. "I think men especially are threatened by me because I'm muscular, I'm strong, and I'm aggressive," Martina once said. Martina felt misunderstood. "I could never understand it. The press would ask me questions, and I would answer, but the next day it's portrayed as arrogance or bitching or whining." These demoralizing conditions began to wear on Martina, making it easy to understand how she could become distant and aloof at times, needing to seek approval. She was drawn toward people with positive energy from which she could draw.

However, once she found a new source of energy, she moved on. When Martina moves on, she moves quickly. Game, set, match—it's over. Whatever it was that enabled Martina to walk away from her homeland spilled over into her personal life. She was able to walk away from one apparently committed relationship to another, never missing a beat, according to those who were with her. While her friends were left bewildered by her ability to move on and leave the past behind, they should have found this pattern predictable. Martina wears her heart on her sleeve, but once it has been broken, she conceals the pain quickly. This behavior was acquired from adversity, but is kept in place for survival in her very public life.

Life on the Circuit
(Life on the Road
With the Maid
and the Champ)

Whaaaap! Martina gave one last slap—just for good measure—to the large duffel bag which contained a compressed featherbed, down comforter, and pillows that they took with them on their travels. It was a ritual shared by Judy and Martina which they performed each time they packed up their belongings and headed for the next town on the tour. Then the ritual would begin anew when they arrived at the next stop on the circuit, where they would unstuff the duffel containing the comforter, pillows, and featherbed. They placed the featherbed atop the bed mattress, covered it with the comforter, then fluffed the pillows and crawled in. This enabled Martina to sleep on a consistent surface each night, while her nose was filled with the scent of her own bed. This made sense, considering that she and Judy were traveling all year long, and that Martina was a multimillion-dollar tennis conglomerate who needed to be kept as physically and emotionally fit as possible. No wonder that she and Judy wanted to take their own bed and surround themselves with the comforts of home.

"It sounds like it would be a lot of work to carry your bed with you, but we made it easy," Judy recalls, laughing as she talks about packing it up each time. "It took both of us to get the air out of those things. First we'd flop on the bed; then we would try to pack it down and roll it up. We would get most of the air out and help flatten it so that it would fit into the duffel bag. Of course, as soon as we lifted it to begin folding it, the feathers puffed up again. We would attack it, sit on it, stand on it—but inevitably we would end up laughing at ourselves. It brought the kid out in each of us."

Life on the road was anything but glamorous and easy, which made these spontaneous and silly moments small treasures in a life filled with endless business decisions, logistic nightmares, and intense pressures as Martina sought to maintain her number-one status in the game.

Peter Johnson of International Management Group had been Martina's manager for most of her career, but now Judy had become the new kid on the block, the person in charge of getting Martina and her entourage from point A to point B, week in and week out. Johnson advised Judy, "Martina does best when she doesn't have to think about anything but tennis. If she's going in a million different directions and having to think about a million different things, she doesn't do well." Clearly, Martina's companion was expected to make sure that Martina was focused on tennis, with as few distractions as possible.

"After a few months on the tour, I became very good at knowing when and what I could tell Martina," Judy recalls. "Peter would call from Cleveland, needing business answers from Martina, but it was my responsibility to either find out the answers to those questions by calling the people involved, or waiting until Martina was able to unwind for a day and then have her return the calls. We knew each other pretty well, in a relatively short period of time, and she trusted me to answer as many of those questions as possible, without having to trouble her. Most of the things I would save up and talk to her about between tournaments, so that she was always clear on what was going on and the direction it was going. But during the tournaments, we didn't discuss them. I also served as a go-between for Martina and the press.

"Unfortunately," Judy explained, "that kind of waiting for the right time spilled over into our emotional lives as well. I wouldn't upset her with the problems I encountered and solved on my own each day or burden her with the emotional struggle I wrestled with. That was my choice. I didn't want her to have to worry about anything except hitting that tennis ball. That kind of focus produces a great tennis champion but leaves far too little left for the relationship. Shifting gears is something I don't do quickly enough. Martina was better at shifting gears and turning her attention to whatever task was at hand. But then, we were making that easy for her, accommodating her schedule and introducing things at just the right moment. As far as I can see, this was always the procedure when someone lived with Martina. The other person always had to become the one responsible for all the details. Other people were hired to carry out instructions, but the person with whom Martina lived was at the helm. It seemed to work that way until one of us got tired of the responsibility or lack of it."

In Martina's world, life on the road was continually hectic and stressful. For instance, travel plans had to be made two or three months in advance, whenever possible, in order to accommodate Martina's and Judy's dogs—who always traveled with them—and Martina's support staff, which seemed to grow larger in number as Martina grew older and more prominent. But they were all considered family and functioned as a unit. Often these well-made plans needed to be changed at the last minute due to unforeseen problems, such as rain or flight delays.

Judy says, "I'd call to change the flight from Sunday to the following morning and would learn that K.D., Martina's smallest dog, couldn't travel on that flight. Another passenger had a dog on that flight, which meant that K.D. couldn't travel on board with us due to a strict policy enforced by all airline carriers that prohibits more than one dog per flight. I'd have to find another route and change everyone's ticket. This meant that Martina would arrive late to the next tournament, and the van that was supposed to pick us up wouldn't be there. The people waiting for Martina were upset because she would miss social events she had committed to months earlier, and the late arrival meant that hotel reservations needed to be changed. Martina would run to the court and start practicing while I talked to the volunteers and apologized for our late arrival. These people had worked on the tournament for weeks, and now they weren't going to have any time with Martina. They were disappointed, and it was my job to smooth things over."

Once Judy and Martina arrived and got settled in, their daily routine was pretty much the same throughout the tournament. Breakfast was the same each day: cooked whole oats, but cooked just so. They rarely socialized with others during meals and preferred to eat by themselves, for the most part. "By the time I joined her, Martina was very particular about her food," Judy recalls. "Ideally, we tried to get housing with a kitchen so I or some family member could prepare her meals. Often we were able to do that. We packed and carried most of our food with us, but our first priority, when we got to town, was to find the best health-food store. Martina was a well-oiled machine, and eating for her was a matter of making the machine perform well. We ate our meals alone in our house or hotel room. We didn't go out much because the food wasn't healthy enough and people always recognized Martina and wanted to talk or ask for her autograph. So things were better when I cooked."

At hotels, or when there was no kitchen, Judy would give their food supplies to the cook with strict cooking instructions. Sometimes that was effective, but most of the time it was a minor disaster; the cooks would lose the instructions as they changed shifts, or would substitute their own ingredients for the ones supplied to them, even when given strict and specific instructions.

Judy recalls, "One night we sent down a week's supply of oats and told the cook how to prepare them and when to deliver them. The next morning, a young man arrived at 8 A.M. and I let him into the room to set up breakfast. When Martina sat down to eat the oats, she grimaced and told the waiter, 'These aren't right. Go back down and cook some more.' Alas, the cook had already taken the entire two-week supply and cooked them; two vats of oats were sitting in a heated cart next to the breakfast table. I spent the next hour locating and delivering another pound of oats to the cook. They got it right the next time!"

Martina was not always a tyrant about healthy meals. Occasionally the two indulged themselves with junk food. This generally happened in airports while traveling from place to place, they would feast on hot dogs and Dr Peppers. Martina rarely drank soft drinks, but she recognized the need to occasionally take a break from her strict diet. Deprivation was never her goal, and she rarely missed a meal. However, she never returned to her "junk food as an American way of life" days, which had been a consuming passion in her early tours on the circuit.

Soon Judy had adjusted to the rigors of life on the road, but she needed and wanted more companionship with the woman she loved and cherished. Their romance was truncated by the demands of the road, and she grew frustrated by outside influences with Martina. Life simply wasn't as spontaneous or natural as she hoped it would be. "Sometimes I would just break down and say, 'Martina, I really feel like everything is moving too fast around us and we need some time alone.' She was always wonderful about stopping whatever she was doing, and we would sit down and talk. And she made me feel very loved and special. She was wonderful that way—when she had the time and energy."

Still, however much both women might have wanted to carve out and preserve more of their intimate life together, Martina's schedule was rigorous and inflexible beyond belief. Tennis was no longer a game, it was her life. She was obligated to her sport and to her corporate sponsors. In between tournaments, Martina and Judy would travel to various locations where Martina needed to fulfill endorsement commitments. "She owed them X number of days a year, and they could use those days however they wanted," Judy explains. "Generally speaking, it would be a photo session for next year's advertising, but there were also new rackets, new socks, new shoes to try. And she'd have to visit the corporate heads of the company for whom she was a spokesperson and shake hands with them, so she was sure they were still happy. Yonex, her long-standing tennis-racket sponsor, wanted her to play with their new model racket, but she really didn't want to change. She was rich and powerful and could usually negotiate with them about the product. But time was a nonnegotiable issue—she owed them her time. And it all kept her away from home."

Judy speaks fondly of what little amount of time they had to vacation and relax, completely away from the sports world. It was the spring of 1987, just before the Italian Open, when they took a vacation in Venice. "We had managed to carve out four days to ourselves if we stayed in Europe rather than flying back to the U.S. to visit the boys and the animals before a long summer in England. Since the ceremony in Brisbane three years earlier, we hadn't had a moment to relax and celebrate our commitment, so we decided to stay in Venice and do that—renew our vows." Neither of us had to been to Venice, so we experienced everything for the first time—the scenery, the canals, the food—they were all wonderful. And we could be alone. No coaches, no trainers, and no family. Just the two of us.

"In Venice, we did just what we did in Brisbane. We went up to a church, early one morning, walked down to the altar, and renewed our vows. When we came out, the bells chimed again. We absolutely couldn't believe it. I had secretly had a replica of the key ring made that I used as a wedding ring in Brisbane, only this time it was real gold. I slipped it on her finger and we made a new commitment."

Judy marked the event with a large heart, carefully drawn on her calendar. Four days later, they went to Monte Carlo, where Martina played an exhibition match, but between the Italian Open and the French Open, they enjoyed two of the world's most romantic cities. "The vacation was short, but very meaningful. It was one of the few times we had where we were completely alone."

Meanwhile, back on the road, Judy entertained Martina's fans while Martina was busy practicing or warming up for a match. These people felt at ease with Judy, and she enjoyed talking to them when she could. "I felt comradeship with Martina's fans; in particular, I knew Martina really didn't have a lot of time for them. They didn't understand that, and probably never would. When she has the time, she is sweet and wonderful. But when she doesn't, she doesn't. I was more constant—I wasn't going to be cold to them one day, then pleasant the next. That is where I come from. That's my family; that's the way we are. If I'm going to pay attention to you and find you valuable as a human being, then that is going to be every day. It's just how I was brought up. I see the hot and cold traits in the players, but that's because they have so many other things on their minds. Yet Martina's fans didn't always understand that. They felt hurt. If one day she talked to them and then the next day she looked right beyond them, they took it personally, but she didn't mean it that way."

Martina's fans were incredibly loyal and dedicated. During Wimbledon, some would even travel from the United States to see her play. If they couldn't afford Wimbledon tickets, they stayed outside the gates in their cars or in tents they had pitched while waiting in line for several nights, hoping to purchase standing-room-only tickets. If it rained, which usually happens sometime during the fortnight, they would hover over their televisions with an umbrella over their heads. Judy and her mother would try to get a few of them gate passes each day, but even for Martina and her family, tickets were spoken for long before the gates opened each day, and there were no extras available. Judy remembers how Bales sympathized with them. "He felt sorry for them, so he would make sandwiches and tea and take it out to them in their tents. Sometimes he would visit the same people two or three years in a row."

Judy's parents stayed at home during most of the year, but during Grand Slam events they often joined Martina and their daughter. Sarge ran errands and took care of the dogs while Frances cooked and washed and cleaned, allowing Judy to enjoy more of the tournament. After tournaments in Europe, Sarge and Frances would have the responsibility of taking all the luggage Judy and Martina had accumulated back to the States, freeing the two to take off for their annual island retreat in Antigua. There they would meet Eddie and Bales, and the boys' best friends, Dru and Michael. This was a happy experience for all. It was family time—no extras, just Judy, Martina, and the kids.

Sarge and Frances lived with Judy and Martina to provide a stable environment for Bales and Eddie, who stayed with their grandparents while Judy was on the road with Martina. They were always there for the boys and kept the home fires burning. When Judy and Martina returned home, Ma had washed and dried their clothes, had the house in good shape, their business affairs in order, allowing them to walk in as though they had never left.

Regardless of her whereabouts, Judy kept in touch with her sons every day. "They needed the same attention from me that they were used to, and I needed—wanted—to be in their lives in a genuine way. They faxed their homework for me to check, and when they needed help with their papers, I always helped them. Of course, we would talk about the schoolwork first, but that was only a small part of their lives. They were really calling to talk to me about their girlfriends and sports and other events in their lives. They made me laugh. I enjoyed talking over their problems and helping them find solutions. Even homework by fax was fun. It was a long-distance family on school days, and we were together most weekends. It wasn't easy, but we made it work. I was the axle of the wheel for Martina, and everything depended on me turning the wheel. Martina was tired at the end of the day, and just as we'd sit down to dinner, one of the boys would invariably call. I was always pulled in several directions—but somehow I managed to keep things running both for Martina and for the boys."

Judy continued, "Bales joined us, more often than Eddie. He loved to attend the events, and I was delighted to have him along. I would plan to pick him up at the airport, but then, at the last minute, I might be needed at the tournament, or we hadn't yet arrived from our last stop, and a volunteer would collect him. He was young and traveling alone; I would worry about him. I was always relieved to see him when he finally arrived to join us." Once either Eddie or Bales arrived at tournaments, they thoroughly enjoyed the time spent with their mother and Martina. They were with Judy while Martina practiced, and then Martina would join them for meals.

In the early years on the tour, Martina's coach, Mike Estep, and his wife always traveled with them. But two years after Judy arrived, Martina replaced Mike with a new coach, Randy Crawford, and a trainer, Joe Breedlove. After Randy, Martina hired Tim Gullickson, and finally, she hired Craig Kardon as her coach. Add to the mix her osteopath and her masseuse, then combine any of the above—plus a few friends and family members, and you have a group the public called "Team Martina."

Late in the relationship with Judy, Martina was struggling to win Grand Slam tournaments and employed sports therapist Jim Loehr to help her through her matches. She had dropped to number two in the rankings behind Steffi Graff and was unable to break the tie she held with Helen Wills Moody, who had set a record with eight Wimbledon titles between 1927 and 1938. "I never really gave her advice about her career, but I did help her focus on what was missing for her and when," Judy recalled. "But I did know the right questions to ask, so that Martina could find the answers for herself. Sometimes she needed her former trainer Nancy Lieberman (a professional female athlete) to train her, and she knew how to push Martina. Sometimes she needed Dr. Renee Richards, her former coach, a brilliant strategist and renowned eye surgeon, who was gentle with her and helped her build self-confidence. One day after some in-depth discussions, Martina decided she needed the guidance of someone who *really* knew how it felt to win Wimbledon. "There was no one like Billie Jean King to coach her for the tournament she wanted to win more than anything else in her life: a record-breaking ninth Wimbledon," recalled Judy.

Judy continued, "Billie Jean and I were friends, she loved my parents—called them Ma and Bigs. We joined Billie Jean in Chicago on occasion, and Billie sometimes went to Texas where Martina practiced on courts located close to our house in Fort Worth."

Billie Jean reminded Martina that tennis was a game that she once enjoyed playing. She helped put the fun back in the game and rekindled the spark under her feet. She would shout, "Green feet, Martina!" as a reminder to her that she needed to move with small, quick steps, as she had moved years earlier. Martina had to concentrate on moving now because she was not as quick off the mark. Billie Jean also broke down strokes. They went over them again and again. Martina was such a natural tennis player that her conditioning and strategy were all she needed to work on. Billie Jean wasn't satisfied with Martina. She knew she needed a stronger and more consistent serve, and Billie Jean worked Martina on her strokes constantly to overcome her younger, hard-hitting challengers. Judy, Billie Jean, and Craig Kardon were part of the team assembled to help Martina gain that one elusive ninth title for which she longed.

Meanwhile, Judy and Martina moved everything (except for their offices and a lake-house residence) from Texas to Aspen where they were in the process of building their dream house. They moved into an interim house in the area called Starwood. Aspen was the perfect location for the two. They were surrounded by other tennis players who enjoyed working out in the clean, pristine mountain air. Martina was just another celebrity in a town that knew how to honor privacy. Chris Evert and Andy Mill lived just a minute away.

In the process of building their home, Judy and Martina had hired two friends to oversee the ranch they were building in Aspen and to take care of the horses. The barn was being built and the house was being framed. Judy was working with IMG (Martina's management company), which was taking charge of the project. "We would spend every spare moment in Aspen either skiing or meeting with the architects on the plans for our dream home—the place where we would retire and ski and ride horses and write our memoirs."

Rising Tensions

On Saturday, July 8, 1990, in the women's final at Wimbledon's center court, Martina reached the pinnacle of her career by defeating Zina Garrison and earning a record ninth singles title, breaking her tie with Helen Wills Moody. On that surprisingly sunny afternoon in England, Martina had become the champion of champions, the best tennis player ever to set foot on the unpredictable and challenging grass courts. She captured the world's most prestigious title with great dedication and skill—and a bit of luck, since her side of the draw had been made easier by Zina Garrison's victories over rising young star Monica Seles and top-seeded Steffi Graff.

Martina had come to Wimbledon on a high note, buoyed by her first visit to Czechoslovakia since the fall of Communism, and only the second trip home for her since her defection in 1975. The contrast between Martina's first return in 1986, when Martina led the United States to a Federation Cup victory, and her second visit, in 1990, was remarkable. She had evolved from the status of "nonperson" to a sanctioned national sports hero in a span of just four years. Judy recalled the first visit in 1986. "The KGB followed us everywhere, and no one was allowed to even say Martina's name. When she played a match against Hana Mandlikova, a fellow Czech, the announcer, following political protocol, introduced Martina as a 'top-ranked player from the United States.' Mandlikova, Martina's brave opponent, also Czech, refused to play until they announced Martina by name. She threw down her racket and encouraged the crowd to put pressure on the announcer. The crowd cheered when Martina Navratilova's name was finally announced over the speakers." It was clear by their reception that the people's hearts and hopes could easily penetrate any wall the government might place between them and Martina. She had her freedom and they didn't. They were not only applauding a great tennis player, but also the very thing which she represented: freedom.

The second visit occurred between the Italian Open and the Pelkington tournament in late April 1990. In Prague and Revnice, Martina and Judy were greeted by smiling citizens with revolutionary optimism. The Communist government had just been overthrown. Weeks earlier, the streets had been filled with strong men and women willing to die for their cause. This was the beginning of a new era, the oppressive "timelessness," imposed by Communist rule was slipping away, and people hungry and eager for their freedom spoke openly about their political beliefs. Symbols of the revolution filled Prague; monuments were erected to honor the new heroes, and flowers were placed in Saint Wenceslas Square each day to mourn those who had been shot down in the streets. People were turning to Vaclav Havel as a leader, a poet and playwright who would soon lead the transition from communism to capitalism through a free election. People's faces reflected their new sense of freedom. The reality of their financial struggle and possible division of the country was still months away.

Martina's name had been erased from record books years earlier when she was denounced as a traitor—a "nonperson," but now her name was restored to record books and her picture placed on the walls of sports clubs. She once more regained her recognition as a valuable part of Czechoslovakian sports history. She was now free to come and go as she pleased; the negative consequences of her defection to America had been erased by a pardon she was granted by the new liberal government. Her fellow Czechs would soon gain access to her through televised matches and learn all about the remarkable career which had been kept from them by their government as much as possible. It was a special time for Martina, and somehow her self-given label of "ex-Czech" seemed like a dusty old concept. Like many of us, Martina was philosophically embracing the idea that the world economy and culture were moving toward a more united world, dependent on each other's resources and enriched by each other's beliefs and values.

Martina and Judy met Havel in person while in Prague on a visit to the castle housing the office of the president. They happened to see him when they simultaneously entered a nearby restaurant for lunch. Introductions were made amid security service men and bodyguards. Havel then invited Martina to speak to the Czech people who were gathered in St. Wenceslas Square, as it was the six-month anniversary of the Velvet Revolution. Thousands of people were awaiting this event, and Martina was given a chance to speak her heart to the people of her homeland. The occasion was overwhelming. As she stood on the balcony she addressed more than 200,000 of her countrymen in their native tongue. They cheered and welcomed her home, and as she addressed them, she hesitated, and said, "I am overwhelmed. I will cry if I continue," She had taken her rightful place in sports history as she addressed the warriors of the Velvet Revolution.

In a more personal moment, when Martina returned with Judy to her hometown of Revnice, they visited the gravesite of Martina's cherished grandmother, who had died several years earlier while Martina was in the United States. Martina rarely speaks about her publicly. However, she and Judy often talked about her grandmother's passing, and both were eager to visit her final resting place. During this trip to Prague, Martina and Judy had walked to the area of the cemetery, where her grandmother's ashes had been spread. There Martina visibly displayed her sorrow and loss which was compounded by the fact that she had missed the earlier ceremony by defecting. She knelt quietly with Judy, and they both wept softly. Judy recalled, "No one will ever share those moments with Martina. We gathered a few pieces of grass and a stone and I picked a tiny purple pansy from the area where her grandmother's ashes had been spread, and Martina took them all with her. We had talked about Martina's home and her grandmother. We just never imagined that we would ever be there together, sharing these most tender and spiritual moments, in a country that was, at last, free. Martina was their hero, and Martina's hero was her grandmother."

While on the trip, Martina and Judy were met by Jana, Martina's younger sister, who had been living in West Germany. This added to the depth and joy of the experience. Martina's mother didn't expect Jana to visit because, prior to the revolution, Jana had been barred from returning. This reuniting experience was indeed a most moving time for the entire Navratil family.

Two months later, Martina reached the finals at Wimbledon. With this, her life seemed to be in complete balance. She appeared radiant as she took center court that Saturday afternoon. She had come a long way from her first Wimbledon victory in 1978 when she was the heavy, dark-haired girl called "the great wide hope." Now she was thirty-four years old, blond, well groomed, with a nearly perfect body, and she exuded confidence. Zina Garrison could not stop a determined Martina from her ultimate goal, and in a historic match, Zina's upset run was finished, as Martina won easily, 6–4, 6–1.

The moments following that final were quite possibly the best moments of Martina's professional life. In that internationally televised ten minutes, after she accepted her place in history, with the decorum of a champion, she savored the moment gracefully. Overwhelmed by the occasion—but still responding with the dramatic flair—she dazzled us with her spontaneous behavior. She held nothing back, showed no awkward doubts about herself, and displayed no unseemly bravado. In those moments, Martina Navratilova was more than a great champion, she was a gracious human being, refusing to be defined by sound bites and clever phrases designed by publicists and managers. She was elegant.

Martina's victory had little or nothing to do with tennis and had everything to do with the heart, soul, and passion displayed by the triumph of the underdog. Martina had fought for years to win the hearts of her fans, and she had proved herself worthy of their loyalty. She possessed the courage needed for such ambitious aspirations and then held fast to the vision and discipline required to achieve such a dream. Martina's achievement served as a reminder that some fantasies are merely visions meant to be realized. As we watched her move beyond her fears, we were all awakened to the ever-expanding potential within each of us, which we might tragically ignore or simply never acknowledge, as we moved through nondescript, flat passages of our lives.

Staring out from a suspended window of disbelief, some hoped silently that Martina might have at least one more Wimbledon title in her, that she might do it again someday. With clearer vision, however, it was obvious that Martina's career had reached its crescendo. There was no way to capture it before it slipped away, no way to stop it and hold it as it merely passed before us. Even those who harbored their doubts in silence, believed that there would be no brighter moment, no clearer sign, no better fanfare for Ms. Navratilova. It was like watching the sun pass below the line of the horizon. Where once there was a brilliant warm mass of energy, now there only remained a few high, thin clouds, streaking a blue-gray sky, reflecting the vibrancy of that which had passed.

As always, Martina's emotions were easy to read. All watching felt her joy as her lips touched the giant Wimbledon trophy and she proudly raised it above her head. She might win one more, but its significance would pale by comparison. Martina had nothing more to prove; she was in a class by herself. As the tears ran down her face, she must have seen, from the corner of her eye, the afternoon shadow which elongated her image as it followed behind her, making her appear larger than life, and reminding onlookers that images become slightly distorted just before they fade and then finally disappear.

Now Martina was about to enter a new phase in her life. In hindsight, it seemed that while sharing parts of her personal world with us, she was marching toward retirement where she would share her life with close friends, but not with the world. Her naïve trust of the press and her honest belief that Americans could embrace her free-spirited nature were now a thing of the past. She was sophisticated and wise to the ways of the world. Perhaps she no longer had a burning desire to be loved and understood by the public at large. She had become a little more clever and a lot less bold. She was in that short space of time after growing up and before growing old. On that day in London, it seemed as though Martina moved from one stage of her life to the next—in an instant.

After the closing ceremony, Martina's family and friends ran back to the house and prepared for her entrance. Judy walked by Martina's side. They were surrounded by guards, the press, and plenty of fans; and, as they came to the gate, Martina was showered with champagne and flowers.

Later, Martina and Judy, along with Rosie Casals, Chris Evert, Billie Jean King, Andrea Jaegar, Gigi Fernandez, Julie Anthony, Craig Kardon, and other close friends went to London for Chinese food. "We had a blast," Judy recalls. "For about four hours we all ate and drank ourselves silly. We were seated in a downstairs area of the restaurant. Everyone was in the mood to just let go after all the hard work. We knew she could do it, and it was wonderful to see her so happy with herself and with her tennis. We had put all our focus on trying to help her achieve this victory. At that moment, all the effort had paid off—no one could ever take this away from her, and we were overjoyed."

Still, something unusual had occurred that afternoon when Martina climbed into the stands and openly embraced Judy and her coaches after her win. It was as if Martina was punctuating the moment or signaling the end of the process. There was just a trace of sadness in her eyes as she headed for the stands that day. Perhaps she might have sensed she needed to express her gratitude, before ending it. It was as though acknowledging their contributions publicly would somehow be her best and only way to show them that she appreciated all their efforts. She was destined to remove herself from the Nelson family in seven months. With her ninth title now behind her, she was able to face personal changes in her life without the fear that these changes would take her focus off her goal. Soon, the reality of a dying relationship—and a clothing business venture that never matured—would come to the forefront, clouding these joyous times.

Judy and her family had loved Martina the best they could, and it had come so easy with her. Even as she played for her ninth Wimbledon title she wore a tennis outfit Judy had designed according to her specifications: soft fabrics, pleated front panel on the skirt, with short sleeves and collar on the shirt. Judy's mother had sewn them for Martina. Frances even washed her clothes for her the night before the final and ironed them as she had done hundreds of times before. Earlier that year, Frances stayed up all night prior to a match and, on her portable sewing machine finished Martina's clothes in time for her match. "I just wanted her to look terrific, and she did," Frances explained. Martina, Judy, and Frances were forced to design clothes for Martina when she was between clothing endorsements in 1989, when her Puma contract expired. Judy remembers the humiliation Martina felt when she failed to get an endorsement immediately. "She was a top player, and she had nothing to endorse. We decided that we could make our own line. It was incredible to me that she was having a hard time getting an endorsement. I felt terrible for her. It wasn't fair." There were times when Frances's finger bled from sewing, by hand, the clothes that Martina wore from 1989 to 1992. For her efforts, Frances held one-quarter interest in MN, a tennis clothing line that did not survive the breakup.

Martina would not simply walk away from her longtime companion and friend, she was leaving a family and children, as well as a business. And at the center of all these worlds was Martina.

After the Wimbledon high, a tennis letdown was inevitable. It showed at the next Grand Slam tournament, the U.S. Open in late August, where Martina, in her own words, "Got my butt kicked in the round of sixteen." She was the number-two seed, but she was hindered by aching knees, and no one was surprised at her poor performance. She continued to play a few tournaments, hoping to finish the year at the Virginia Slims championships at Madison Square Garden in New York, but she was forced to withdraw just days before the matches in November. Surgery was scheduled for December.

Martina's physical woes heightened the increasingly stressful relationship with Judy. On the business side, the MN clothing line was about six months late for its scheduled release, and Judy and Martina were busy in New York working out distribution and shipping plans with the Herman Geist company. Orders were coming in from all over the country, but production problems in Argentina slowed things down. The clothing line, like all projects, added stress to the relationship. IMG was intervening, causing disquieting discussions about fair distribution of profits among Judy, Martina, and Frances. Everyone's roles and responsibilities were clearly defined, but the value of the role was not individually appreciated. IMG tried to draw up the contracts to everyone's satisfaction, but Judy and Frances still felt compromised or devalued by the final terms. It wasn't so much a financial issue, but suddenly, by defining the value of each person's contribution, a stratification solidified in their minds. Basically, Martina's name was more valuable than their time and effort. What for years had been seen as egalitarian relationships among them had now been defined contractually as hierarchical, with Martina's price of endorsement nonnegotiable and clearly more valuable to the company. This new structure, demanded by IMG, definitely changed the way the family would relate to one another in the future.

Still, outward optimism was certainly present. By all public appearances, the atmosphere seemed to be fine. Judy and Martina were busy promoting the clothing line together. Martina made a guest appearance on David Letterman's late-night show to plug the products, and Judy planned with Ivana Trump for a special gala party and preview at the Plaza Hotel in New York. Both couples (Judy and Martina and Ivana and Donald) were about to fall apart at the seams, but fashion and social life were all part of business and pleasure and, by all appearances, life continued as usual.

Judy says she never saw it coming—the end of the relationship with Martina. "I just didn't think she would leave me. I thought she adored me," Judy confessed. "I learned the hard way that anyone can leave anybody." Every relationship has its ups and downs and Judy believed that she and Martina would be together forever, despite signs to the contrary. She had only her marriage by which to gauge the seriousness of the situation, and ultimately it was she who insisted on the divorce. Judy had never been left (abandoned for a time, but never left without the possibility that her loved one would eventually return). When she first became friends with Martina, she anticipated that Martina would have access to many women, and that concerned her at first. This, coupled with Martina's youth and endless opportunities, forced Judy to conclude that there was at least a good possibility they would experience some rough times during a lifetime together. But, as the years passed, Judy felt increasingly comfortable and secure. However, these anticipated problems, once pointed out and dealt with, would be resolved, and their lives would continue, as promised. In Judy's mind, it was all part of the process, and nothing more. What was perceived by others as the beginning of the end was perceived by Judy as little more than a rough period to be weathered. But, if Judy had no idea what was happening with Martina, their Aspen friends seemed to know better.

Serious trouble in the relationship actually began to surface about two years earlier, in the winter of 1988/1989, when Judy recognized that Martina was developing what others believed was "more than a friendship" with a ski instructor in Aspen. Martina rode the gondola up the mountain for the final run of the day with the instructor, leaving Judy behind. These gondola rides were cozy and intimate, holding only the two women as they relaxed before taking an invigorating last run. Meanwhile, Martina gave her new friend a diamond necklace for Christmas, and people close to the women were beginning to talk about a possible breakup. According to Judy, rumors circulated, but a relationship never developed.

When Judy questioned Martina about her feelings for this woman, the questioning led to several serious discussions about their own relationship. This style of communication "processing" was Judy's bread-and-butter approach to problem solving and self-discovery. It was also consistent with Judy's and Martina's beliefs that through communication they could resolve their problems. Martina and Judy had an oral agreement between them about how they would deal with romantic distractions. There was always a commitment to monogamy, but at the same time an understanding that there would be times when either might find someone else attractive. They believed that if they were direct and honest about their distractions, they would be able, through discussions, to "work it out." This process seemed to work for them. The assumption was that if one were attracted to someone outside the relationship, then something inside of it was not serving them. By talking about the distraction they would be able to articulate their fears and needs and allow themselves an opportunity to meet those needs. The obvious flaw in this strategy was that the conversations took place too late in the game.

The Nelson-Navratilova family had been intact for five years. Judy and Martina, Judy's two sons, and Judy's parents, Frances and Sargent Hill had been living together in Texas and Judy and Martina had just moved to Aspen, full time. Eddie, Judy's elder son, continued living with his father most of the time throughout Martina and Judy's relationship but Bales, who for all those years had lived with Judy and Martina, had chosen to remain in Texas to finish out his high-school years with his friends and classmates. From 1984 to 1989, Judy and Martina lived in Fort Worth near Ed Nelson so that the two young boys could move freely between the two houses.

"We had always planned to move to Aspen when Eddie went to college," Judy remembered, "but when it actually came time to move and Bales wasn't coming with us as we had hoped, it was difficult to leave. But we both loved Aspen and had already begun building the home we thought we would live in forever. As it turned out, it was good for Bales to live with his father. They grew to love and appreciate each other more."

In 1989, when Judy and Martina moved from Fort Worth to

Aspen, Bales decided to remain in Texas with his father. This meant that Judy's parents were free to live where they pleased for the first time since Judy's divorce. They no longer needed to maintain a home for Bales while Judy and Martina were away. Though Judy and Martina asked her parents to join them in Colorado, they declined the invitation, stating that Aspen was "too cold" for them, and they remained in Fort Worth. But Judy had some difficult adjustments to make. She was leaving her hometown, moving several states away from her parents and children.

Up till now the family unit served Martina well. She was enchanted by their Southern charm and kind hearts. Martina seemed to have needed them and Judy, the boys, the pets, and the parents, all seemed happy with the arrangement. They shared one central home (in Texas), occupied by several generations who all worked toward a common cause—in this case, producing a well-polished tennis champion. The tasks were well distributed and, if members of the family were unhappy with the arrangement, no one was aware of it.

The move to Aspen changed the family structure and created an intimate family of two.

Trouble began to brew. Martina's knees were beginning to threaten her game. By December 1990, her world ranking dropped to number two, behind Graf, and her earnings were well below what they had been in the previous four years. Despite Wimbledon, Grand Slam wins had been elusive over the past few years, and she could hear the footsteps of young Argentine player Gabriela Sabatini, who had just won the U.S. Open. Even more impressive was the young Monica Seles, a Yugoslavian who proved she could win a Grand Slam or two herself in both Paris and Australia.

Meanwhile, back in Colorado, Judy and Martina were busy making plans for their beautiful new home on 100 acres high in the mountains of Aspen. The design of this house was radically different from their other houses. Rather than a spacious house with many bedrooms and baths, this structure was designed to enclose large open spaces surrounded by a few large walls. As one entered the expansive living quarters one was struck by the sense of open spaces and wilderness. Windows were strategically placed allowing one to see through the house to the mountains where it lay nestled. Large windows framed the trees and the snowcapped mountains. The structure itself was elegant and open, the rooms designed to allow in as much of the outside as possible. It was a dream house, with no room for guests. Judy and Martina intended to keep their house near Independence Pass. They planned to have room to accommodate their family and friends, but after years of living with others, this house and this time would belong only to them. The house was designed for one couple and was a sharp contrast to the Starwood house with its five bedrooms and five baths. They were preparing for retirement, when they would be able to enjoy their home together.

Retirement, for Martina, in 1990, was perhaps a fear rather than a dream. For the first time in her career, she seemed frightened and vulnerable. Her game, which requires tremendous speed to reach the net quickly, assuring dominance in a serve-and-volley game, was slowing down. Martina needed to make adjustments in her game and to change some of her own expectations about her performance capabilities. Billie Jean King was working on her attitude, keeping her in a positive state of mind, while reminding Martina that she needed to think about moving her feet more. What was natural in her twenties was something she had to focus on now.

In early December Martina underwent knee surgery in Vail, Colorado, a town about 100 miles east of Aspen. While recovering from the surgery, she was unable to work out. For several weeks during the recovery process, she had no sure way of knowing whether or not the operation was successful. Dr. Steadman, her surgeon, assured her that the operation had gone well and that she would be as good as ever, but until she actually tested them out, she could only hope and trust that her legs would again serve her well. At this point, neither Judy nor Martina knew whether Martina would be able to play professional tennis at the same level again. Martina planned to play tennis for a few more years. She needed to continue winning in order to develop the ranch and finish building the home they had designed. Beyond the monetary hopes, Martina was chasing a few more titles. She was only a few victories shy of Chris Evert's record of 157 singles titles.

The surgery was an unqualified success. Martina recovered and was rehabilitating herself over the Christmas holidays. Martina's sister Jana, along with her boyfriend and Martina's parents, were visiting for Christmas. Judy and her family were there, too. It was during this time, after the turmoil of many guests over the holidays, that Judy was awakened in the night several times with bad stomach cramps. She was hospitalized for tests on New Year's Eve. As it turned out, the pains stemmed from a spastic colon, which was a condition that Judy developed two years earlier as a result of stress. It just happened that this time the pains were so severe that a visit to the emergency room was necessary in order to get some relief. The doctors also needed to be certain that it was Judy's colon problem alone that was causing the pain.

Martina was less than attentive to Judy while she was hospitalized and seemed to care more about skiing than playing nurse. The day Judy came home from the hospital, Martina was out with her friends on Vail Mountain. Initially, Judy was understanding. Martina had gone to Vail for a checkup on her knees, and appointments were not that easily worked into her schedule. Martina wanted to know about her own progress and while Judy was upset that she would schedule an appointment for that day, she understood Martina's concern about her recovery. Judy didn't understand that skiing was part of the day's activities. The fact that Martina was skiing, when Judy was just coming home, upset her. As Judy waited for her to call, in between runs (which she failed to do), she became even more hurt and angry. This was a relationship built on constant communication; for Martina not to phone meant she was distracted, and that's how Judy interpreted it. When Martina finally did call Judy, Judy told her, "We need to talk about what is happening to our relationship, or lack of one."

Judy was hurt by Martina's apparent disregard for her, and her lack of attention. Martina was unwilling to meet Judy's needs. Rather than express her anger toward Martina, Judy became hurt and depressed. The two had long talks after Martina returned from Vail. There was no major blowup or long argument. But emotions had shifted. Martina seemed at a distance to Judy.

Judy was afraid that perhaps Martina had found someone else, creating a situation similar to the one that had occurred two years earlier. Martina again denied any such feelings and made an effort to make Judy feel comfortable and happy again. "We had both been under a great deal of stress," Judy recalled. "We had a house full of family and friends over the holidays. I had been sick enough to be hospitalized twice in less than a week, and Martina was not sure that she could ever play the quality of tennis that had kept her ranked as the number one or two player in the world for a decade.

"With this in mind, we tried to think about the upcoming tournament, and put our fears aside. Martina, I think, was always better at this than me. I was not accustomed to hiding my feelings. But there was no time for personal considerations— there was a tournament to play, and a number-one ranking to regain. There were still more records to be broken, too. Besides, Martina did most of her confronting on the tennis court and had very little of herself left to face on an emotional, personal level. She was great at simply adjusting and acting like nothing had ever happened. Nothing, that is, until *she* has made a decision. When Martina has decided to say goodbye, she doesn't look back. At least it seemed that way to me. Her pattern in the past proves my theory correct."

A new tennis season was about to start in mid-January, however, with Tokyo the first tournament stop. As a tune-up, Martina went to Chicago to work with Billie Jean King and her coach Craig Kardon. Judy would join her in a few days. Before leaving, Martina left a Post-It note on the mirror that said,

"Judy, I miss you already. I love you madly and I can't wait to see you."

Judy arrived in Chicago with high hopes, but soon sensed a change of climate for the worse. She tried to talk again with Martina about her insecurities, but Martina wasn't interested; this discussion was fairly brief, and Martina left to go to practice.

After Martina left the room, Judy did something that she justifies by saying that she simply had to find out if Martina was actually interested in another woman. From Billie Jean King's house, Judy sent a fax to a person she thought could offer some answers. The fax read, "I am here. You can fax me if you like. No one will see it, signed, "M." The recipient, who was probably unfamiliar with Martina's handwriting, was fooled into thinking that anything she faxed Martina was for her eyes only. Yet there was Judy, at the fax machine, watching and reading the pages as they came in.

When Martina returned to the house, Judy approached her with the ill-gotten fax. "I told her how I had gotten the fax. That I had lied, and led this person to believe that she was faxing Martina. She was not amused. In fact, she was furious. I know she had the right to be, but I told her that given the same situation, I would probably do it all over again. I did, however, insist on calling the person that evening to confess what I had done. That did not make it right, though, and it never will."

The two had a painful conversation. Martina confessed to Judy that she was falling out of love with her. Judy had successfully forced a small confrontation between them, but Martina felt betrayed by this act. Judy was filled with remorse. Yet despite all the anguish this caused, the bottom line reality was that Martina was about to head out again on tour—testing the success of her knee surgery and rehabilitation—and the two women both knew they must bracket their emotions and postpone any serious confrontation until a later day. So even though Judy was ambivalent about flying to Tokyo (the last tournament she would attend as Martina's partner and would have preferred to stay in Aspen) she knew it was important to be there. At this point the relationship was held together by a thread, but Judy refused to contemplate a breakup. She held on to the hope that conditions would turn around. "How could she adore me one moment and then leave me the next?" she wondered.

Martina played remarkably well in Japan, though she lost to Sabatini in a three-set final. On the flight home, Judy noticed that Martina was entering long passages in her journal, but concealed her curiosity and doubts by turning her back and falling asleep.

Judy's parents were at the Starwood house when they returned from Japan. As usual, Judy went upstairs and began to unpack their bags. Meanwhile, Martina uncharacteristically went downstairs to Judy's office on the second level of the house. Judy and her mother walked into the office (to go through important mail and packages) at the precise moment that Martina was faxing pages of her journal to someone. Martina sat at Judy's desk, watching the pages as they were being transmitted. Judy became consumed with doubt and suspicion. For a moment she froze, then realized what was happening. Frightened, she felt her self-esteem melting away. She knew this couldn't continue. She then turned and left with her mother.

A few minutes later, from the third level of the house, an odd thing happened. Judy's mother turned to her and asked, "Ju, do you smell something burning?"

Judy said, "Yes, I'll check it out." She then returned to the office alone and witnessed Martina setting fire to pages of her journal in the trash can, while talking on the phone.

"What are you doing?" Judy asked, enraged.

Martina, sitting next to her flaming trash can, calmly replied, "I'm burning the fax."

"I think we need to talk right now." Judy went upstairs and waited for Martina.

When Martina entered the room, Judy said, "Martina, if you are not in love with me, you cannot stay in this house. You have to leave this house now, tonight. This is too painful. It is killing me. We both need some time and space to work through all of this."

"Where will I go?" Martina replied. "It's the middle of the night. Can I just sleep in another room?"

"No, you have to leave. You can go up to the ranch. You can't stay here with me when you feel that you are in love with someone else."

As Martina left the bedroom, Judy added, "You have to wake Ma and Bigs and tell them that you are leaving. They are not aware that anything is wrong, and they deserve an explanation."

Martina resisted initially, but Judy insisted upon it. Martina and Judy walked into the bedroom to wake Judy's parents. "Mother, Dad, Martina is leaving, and she needs to talk to you," Judy said in a quivering and tearful voice.

"No, that's all right, we can do it later," Martina said.

But Judy's mother, even in her sleepy state realizing that something was terribly wrong, got up and went into the living room with her daughter and Martina. Judy was crying when Ma asked, "Martina, why are you leaving?"

"Ma, I can't love Judy the way she needs to be loved. So I have to go now."

Ma, too, began to cry. As Judy and Ma held each other, Martina got her skis and bags and put them in her red Ford Explorer, and drove away.

It would be a week before Martina returned to the house. She left town to play an exhibition match and then returned home for her belongings. During this time, Judy and Martina saw each other only when Martina had to repack her bags. Judy never dreamed, when she asked Martina to leave that night of February 3, that Martina would never sleep in that house again. She hoped that Martina, after some reflection, would return to her.

The Event

Despite efforts by the family to downplay the issue, Judy's and Martina's relationship was political. This was an unsanctioned marriage between two women, and while their union may have mirrored heterosexual institutions, it was not recognized as legitimate by the state of Texas or by social norms. Thus, when their relationship came apart in 1991, the two women found themselves embroiled in a nasty legal battle in Texas, where homosexuality is illegal and community property is not guaranteed, even in marriage.

In that environment, Judy was forced to ask the state to honor a nonmarital partnership agreement that ostensibly established Judy and Martina as business partners and outlined how the couple's assets would be distributed at the end of the relationship. Unfortunately for Judy, she already had two legal strikes against her, litigating in a state where the law was hostile toward gays and toward women.

The Nelson-Navratilova dispute centered on an agreement that was signed in Texas in 1986, almost a year after Judy's divorce from Ed Nelson was finalized. While the document was never truly tested, it stated that Judy and Martina would split all earnings made by either or both women while they were living together. The document itself is formal, but, according to BeAnn Sisemore, it was actually drawn up from a document book. BeAnn had also incorporated notes given her by Judy and Martina.

Starting with the Brisbane ceremony in 1984, what appears to be a straightforward series of casual linear actions would become, in Martina's mind, evidence of a conspiracy put in place and carried out by Judy and her family—a plan to emotionally entrap her into turning over millions of dollars to Judy. On the other hand, Judy countered with a videotape of the contract-signing event as evidence that Martina had acknowledged and participated in their mutual effort to clarify their business partnership in writing.

The sequence of events that occurred during the contract-signing process the evening of February 12, 1986, in Fort Worth remain in dispute. The videotape fails to support either side in a clear, cogent, and convincing manner. After examining the actions of the people present that evening, and after viewing the videotape, one soon realizes: if either side relies on a jury to interpret this videotape in isolation, many years after the fact, it will be at the mercy of their attorney's ability to direct and manipulate the perceptions of those individuals in the jury box. The superior attorney will pick out isolated moments that either support the client's position, or place doubt in the jury's mind about the opponent's integrity, clarity, or intent. Due to the emotional charge created by both allegations—Martina's conspiracy charge against Judy and Judy's "breach of contract with intent to deceive" charge against Martina—cleverness on the part of their counsel could easily eclipse any simple interpretation of evidence and testimony given in court on any given day.

Simply stated, this legal document and videotape do little more than prove that Nelson and Navratilova were in the same room together and that they signed a document that was especially designed for them and by them. This "evidence" doesn't provide enough information about the three most salient issues. First, did the document accurately reflect their intentions, designed by both over a two-year period? Second, had Martina read and reviewed the document at least once before the taping? And third, if the document truly failed to represent Martina's wishes, why did she never make an effort to nullify the agreement during the five-year period that followed?

What the videotape does do is offer concrete information

about what was said during the process of entering into the formal contract and the playful spirit of those who participated in "The Event" that evening.

Martina had come home in the late afternoon, after playing basketball with Nancy Lieberman. Her mother and her sister Jana were visiting, and Judy's parents were preparing a festive dinner. One of the guests was BeAnn Sisemore, the paralegal who first spent time with Judy and Martina at Wimbledon in 1984 and had since become a good friend to both women. She would bring along the partnership contract she had typed for them to sign. No one was really aware that this "event" would happen sometime that evening. Whatever, it would be a private signing between Judy and Martina. Judy's brother Sarge would videotape the event, but it would take place upstairs, away from the family. Just as they had done earlier, when they made their commitment to each other in Brisbane, Judy and Martina did not want their families to witness something that was meant to be private. Little did they imagine that the videotape would end up on national television five years later.

Before the signing took place (but with the video camera off), Martina was allegedly asked to review the contract. Sarge also took photographs of Martina on the floor next to the contract, before shooting the video. According to Judy, she had access to the contract prior to signing, yet she would later testify in court that she had not read the agreement. People who know Martina acknowledge that she can be less than thorough when it comes to reading contracts. She generally relies upon the expertise of people she employs and trusts to take on that responsibility. Therefore, the photograph of the contract lying beside her seems to prove no more than the possibility that she was given the time and the opportunity to go over the details. Martina contends that she did not go over the contract at that time. It does seem to support Judy's position that she wasn't trying to "pull something over" on Martina by confronting her with an unfamiliar document at the last moment.

The videotape was shot in Bales's bedroom and runs about twenty minutes. Judy and Martina are shown sitting next to each other in gold plastic chairs, with BeAnn in front of them, holding an original of the document. BeAnn introduces the proceeding as "The Event," even using a slapboard, and a movie reference is made. She tells the camera, "You must understand this is not Martina's first television experience, but it is for Judy." She continues, "We are here at 708 Roaring Springs Road, and the reason we are here is because Judy and Martina want to sign an agreement that makes them partners in whatever they do financially, like they have been partners for almost two years." Throughout this process the cat, Lancelot, and a dog, K.D., roam through the picture. Each woman picks up the animals, and they joke about Judy's kids not being tax deductible.

The purpose of the tape is to witness the signing of the agreement. To this end, each page is signed by Judy and Martina, with Martina pointing out little errors in the document and even the places where Judy needs to sign or initial. The tape ends with a slap of the studio board and Judy and Martina exchanging "high fives."

Judy and Martina each receive an original copy of the document and are warned by BeAnn that they cannot keep it in Jerry Loftin's office, but are solely responsible for its safekeeping. According to Judy, one copy is later given to their secretary to be put in the safe at the office of Jim Shaffer, their financial adviser at the time. Martina disputes Judy's account of the document's path. In her version, somewhere and sometime in the process Loftin saw or handled the document. Judy and BeAnn swear he didn't. Its path remains in dispute. The other copy is placed in a safe in the closet upstairs. This document will be moved to Aspen in 1988 and stored in the same safe in a closet in the Starwood house. The other copy will eventually be sent to IMG with Judy and Martina's other financial records when they change financial advisers.

Why did they name this ritual "The Event"? It was clearly not a marriage ceremony, and it lacked any kind of romance in its structure. Also, why were their parents not invited into the room as witnesses? And, if it was a "business partnership agreement," why were no attorneys present?

To explore these questions, we must look at two specific elements of this event: namely, the signing itself and the contract. The fact that neither, in this context, is rich in legal tradition means that neither party can rely ultimately upon interpretations based on long tradition, such as traditional marriage contracts or business partnerships. Retroactively reconstructing the event for the purpose of a legal battle will fail because neither side can look to "social norms" for interpretation of intent and meaning.

Judy explains that her parents were not in the room because she and Martina wanted an informal and private environment for what they regarded as a private event. This seems consistent with the relationship that the two women had with her parents. Judy's father has often asserted that he and Frances do not get involved in their children's private matters (which may help explain why their marriage is intact after fifty years). Yet one is left wondering why a videotape would be regarded as private when shot in front of Judy's brother and BeAnn. In theory, of course, a videotape is neutral and concrete, without bias or prejudice, yet even these accounts are subject to a viewer's bias and prejudice. Suffice to say, Judy and Martina wanted to have a private event, and they kept it that way.

A much more important question remains: Why were no attorneys involved at any stage during this process? It seems inconceivable, at first, that either woman would enter into a business agreement of this consequence without serious legal counsel. Otherwise, working against social norms, without legal counsel, each person was left vulnerable to individual interpretation of meaning. The fact that this document was never evaluated as to its legitimacy or its legal viability meant that the people signing it never truly understood the consequences for ultimately not honoring it.

Of course, Martina could be credited with greater shrewdness than she seemed to exhibit here. A pessimistic interpretation is that perhaps she never felt seriously obligated to something that was not recognized by the state of Texas as litigious. Given that this contract and the signing lacked tradition, the videotape either supports Martina's alleged confusion or leaves open the possibility that she entered into the agreement promising generosity while both social norms and legal traditions would allow her a great deal of maneuvering. One would then conclude that this document was intended to be used as a negotiation tool rather than one which Judy would seek to have upheld by the state.

In such a theoretical scenario, Martina could be gambling, believing that she would either be with Judy forever, or that in the unlikely event of a future split, she would win a summary judgment on grounds that an illegal act in Texas (homosexuality) might have taken place (or be promised, implied or expected) in order to fulfill the requirements of carrying out the duties and responsibilities in the contract. One cannot contract to perform illegal acts of any kind and later ask the court to enforce the contract. The contract itself is evidence against you. In *Nelson* v. *Navratilova*, it would be difficult to prove that an "illegal" act hadn't occurred before the two entered into the contract, and that this illegal act didn't, in some emotional way, have some bearing on Martina.

It seems unbelievable to many that this legal argument could still prevail in 1991, and it didn't in most states, but Texas was an exception. In that state, this law could, with a conservative judge or jury, be grounds for dismissal, making the document not worth the paper it had been written on. Therefore, rather than confronting Judy about any inconsistencies about what she actually wanted and those in the agreement, Martina could feel fairly confident that she would be in a strong position to negotiate better terms, should the time come.

In the videotape, BeAnn Sisemore even admits that this procedure is unusual and says, "If anyone has done this before, we sure can't find it." She also warns Judy and Martina: "You have both waived your rights to be represented by an attorney."

Mike McCurly, head counsel for Navratilova, later asserted that this contract was part of a conspiracy against Martina by Judy and her family. In this scenario, Martina was not represented and did not know what she was signing. In court, Martina said that she thought BeAnn was an attorney and was thus protecting her interests. Then, in an interview with *People* magazine in July 1991, Martina said, in response to a motion filed by Judy to uphold this agreement, "I just trusted everybody because here I was with Judy and her lawyer . . . I cannot believe she is doing it for the money."

Opinions about the fairness of the Nelson-Navratilova document vary greatly among the general population and members of the gay community. Sociologist Philip Bloomstein and Pepper Schwartz, in their 1983 book, *American Couples*, report that most people, gay and heterosexual alike, feel that both partners should work and contribute to the household budget. Judy herself undertook a supportive role to Martina, one traditionally held by a wife in marriage. Few feminists argue against the idea of community property for most women who are married, but many feminists support Martina's position: that Judy was not entitled to half of the assets acquired during their relationship.

If women are going to ask for equal rights and protections, they must take equal responsibility. A disservice is done to all women when the value of support work is not recognized. By dismissing nurturing, we fail to give incentive to our children to grow up as caring people. Vision and consistency are lacking when a double standard is used for men and women; what is good for the goose is good for the gander, and vice versa.

Now, turning attention to content, is the Nelson-Navratilova agreement fair? Here's a copy for the reader to read and interpret.

A friendly game of tennis: "Lady and the Champ," 1988.

A family Christmas in Fort Worth, 1988: Martina and Judy with Judy's sons, nieces, and nephews.

Judy with the animals:
a picnic with the dogs
in Italy, 1989.

Judy's prize 1987
birthday gift from
Martina: a champion
saddle horse from
Kalorama Farm
selected by Rita Mae
Brown to give to Judy.

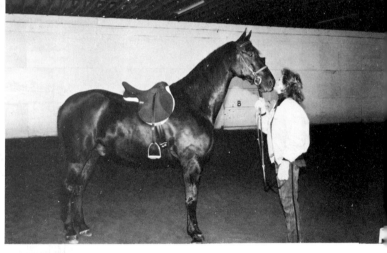

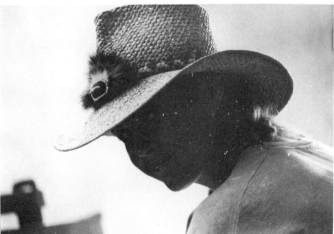

Martina's favorite photo
of Judy. (Martina took it.)

At home on the range in
Aspen: Martina and Judy
on their quarter horses.

Martina's workout regime--basketball.
(Judy gives tips?)

In the "players box" at Wimbledon:
Judy and mother Frances, in 1989.

Judy and family at Virginia Slims championships in New York, 1989: Sarge, Jan, Judy, Sargent, and Frances.

Brother and sister? No, Just Martina and Judy's son Eddie in Aspen, 1990.

On a visit to Martina's namesake, a ski lodge called Martinova in Czech: Bud Collins, Judy, and Martina.

Martina, before addressing 200,000 people in Wenceslas Square, Prague, on the six-month anniversary of the Velvet Revolution.

Judy and Bales celebrating a victory at Wimbledon in 1990.

The victory walk home: Judy and Martina returning to their rented house at Wimbledon just after Martina's historic ninth Wimbledon victory.

Wimbledon victory party, 1990: A fun evening for close friends Dr. Judy Anthony, Judy, Martina, and Andrea Jaeger.

Surprise victory party atop Aspen Mountain after Wimbledon in 1990. Judy and Martina arrive for a picnic at which the town turned out to applaud the champ.

Dru (the "adopted" son, Bales's best friend), Martina, and Bales at the Aspen ranch, "N2" (Navratilova-Nelson), at Thanksgiving, 1990.

A field of flowers and new hope: Judy's hike to Crested Butte with son Eddie in August 1991.

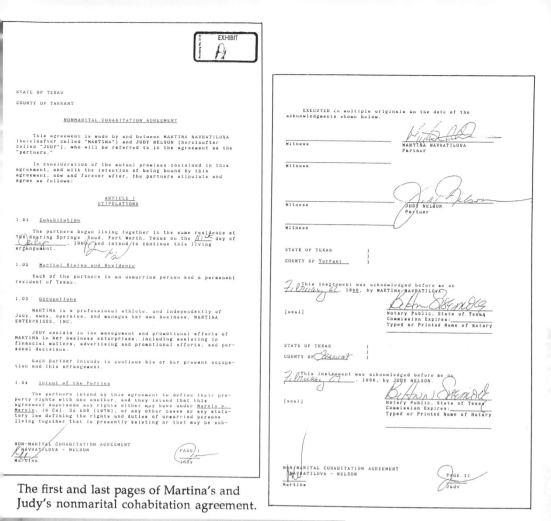

The first and last pages of Martina's and Judy's nonmarital cohabitation agreement.

"The judge—have gavel, will travel" is his motto: Judge Harry Hopkins with members of the foreign press, Fort Worth, Texas, August 1991. (The picture was taken during the hearing on disqualification for Judy's attorney.)

All grown up: Eddie,
November 1991.

Judy Nelson today on her
farm in Virginia.

The end—a new
beginning: Bales, Judy,
Eddy.

STATE OF TEXAS

COUNTY OF TARRANT

NON-MARITAL COHABITATION AGREEMENT

This Agreement is made by and between MARTINA NAVRATILOVA (hereinafter called "MARTINA") and JUDY NELSON (hereinafter called "JUDY"), who will be referred to in the agreement as the "partners."

In consideration of the mutual promises contained in this agreement, and with the intention of being bound by this agreement, now and forever after, the partners stipulate and agree as follows:

ARTICLE 1
STIPULATIONS

1.01   Cohabitation

The partners began living together in the same residence at 708 Roaring Springs Road, Fort Worth, Texas on the _____ day of _____, 1985, and intend to continue this living arrangement.

1.02   Marital Status and Residence

Each of the partners is an unmarried person and a permanent resident of Texas.

1.03   Occupations

MARTINA is a professional athlete, and independently of Judy, owns, operates, and manages her own business, MARTINA ENTERPRISES, INC.

JUDY assists in the management and promotional efforts of MARTINA in her business enterprises, including assisting in financial matters, advertising and promotional efforts, and personal decisions.

AGREEMENT/MARTINA NAVRATILOVA – JUDY NELSON

Each partner intends to continue his or her present occupation and this arrangement.

1.04   Intent of Parties

The partners intend by this agreement to define their property rights with one another, and they intend that this agreement supersede any rights either may have under *Marvin* v. *Marvin*, 18 Cal. 3d 660 (1976), or any other cases or any statutory law defining the rights and duties of unmarried persons living together that is presently existing or that may be subsequently enacted, and to define to the best of their ability their intent on the division of any properties which they may hereafter acquire.

ARTICLE 2
EFFECTIVE DATES

2.01   Effective Dates

This agreement shall be effective as of the 10th day of July, 1984, which is the date that the parties began living together, and shall continue until the separation of the partners or the death of either partner. Separation shall be defined as the date when either party notifies the other in writing that they no longer desire to live together.

ARTICLE 3
PRESENT FINANCIAL POSITION

3.01   Present Financial Position

Each partner has carefully examined the other's financial condition and position. As part of such disclosures, each partner has examined the other's present assets and liabilities as shown on the attached schedules and made all inquiries about the other's assets and liabilities deemed appropriate. Each partner acknowledges receipt of satisfactory information and responses to all such inquiries.

AGREEMENT/MARTINA NAVRATILOVA – JUDY NELSON

ARTICLE 4
SEPARATE PROPERTY

4.01 Assets and Liabilities as Separate Properties

The property described hereinafter will remain the separate property of the partner who is the titleholder, free of any interest, beneficial, equitable, or otherwise, in the other partner:

1. All property, whether real or personal, owned by the respective partner at the effective date of this agreement and so defined in the attached schedules referred to herein.

2. All property acquired by the respective partner out of the proceeds or income from property owned at the effective date of this agreement or attributable to appreciation in value of said property, whether the enhancement is due to market conditions or to the services, skills, or efforts of the owner of the property.

3. All property hereafter acquired by the respective partner by gift, devise, bequest, or inheritance, or income from said property, or attributable to appreciation in value of said property, whether the enhancement is due to market conditions or to the services, skills, or efforts of the owner of the property.

4.02 Earnings as Joint Property

Except as hereinafter provided, the earnings and income of each partner will become the joint property of the partners, and will be subject to division upon separation as defined herein. Further, any property hereafter acquired by either partner out of the earnings or income of either party after the commencement of this agreement, and any income from said property or appreciation in value of said property, whether the enhancement is due to market conditions or to the services, skills, or efforts of either party, will become the joint property of the partners, and the partners shall own same as tenants in common.

AGREEMENT/MARTINA NAVRATILOVA – JUDY NELSON

ARTICLE 5
LIVING EXPENSES

5.01 Provision for Payment of Living Expenses and Purchases
Made from Account

MARTINA and JUDY will pay their expenses while they
are living together from the funds that are earned by either
of them. The monies which either of them may receive as
income will be shared by them jointly and will hereafter be
considered as their joint property to pay for their living
expenses and personal enjoyment while they are living
together. Either party is free to use and enjoy, without any
claim for reimbursement for same from the other any and all
monies which they may desire. Any proceeds remaining from
such earnings of either party after any date in which either
party may desire to terminate this agreement by separation
as provided for hereinabove, shall be the joint proceeds of
the parties, to be equally divided.

It is the intent of this provision to clearly define that
should one party benefit to a greater degree in any or all of
the months in which the parties may live together, the other
party shall not be entitled to a reimbursement for the
difference in the use and enjoyment of such funds at any
future time. Rather, both shall be free to use, enjoy, spend,
save, or otherwise pay for expenses as they arise and should
be needed by either of the respective parties without any
subsequent claim for reimbursement from the other party for
the difference in funds allocated to one or the other during
the period in which they lived together.

Each partner will, from the joint funds thereafter acquired
by them individually or jointly, pay as they are incurred, or
become due, whatever respective personal living expenses they
may each incur, including, but not limited to food, clothing,
travel, entertainment, housing, and the like, with no claim or
entitlement for reimbursement due to the other party for a
like amount not being paid to the other party.

It is not the intention of the parties for each of them to
draw equal amounts on a monthly basis, but instead that

earnings earned by either of them shall be shared and enjoyed or used as needed by each of them throughout the period of time they live together. They likewise would then divide equally any funds or other assets remaining from those acquired after the commencement of this agreement in the event that either party may hereafter desire to separate as defined herein.

The parties may from time to time need money and expense to purchase gifts for or assist in the living expenses of family or friends, and may further have a need for funds to pay for their respective separate property investments. Neither party shall ever claim reimbursement from the other at any time for any funds defined herein as joint monies which may be utilized for these purposes, even though one party or that party's estate or family may have benefited more than the other. It is merely the intention of the partners to live their lives without complication or fear of future litigation for reimbursement or sums that could be construed to be due to the other and to forever settle such unanticipated dispute by agreement herein.

The partners may from time to time make gifts to the other party of certain items. That gift shall remain the separate property of the person receiving the gift, and shall forever be free from the claim of the other partner.

Each partner will file his or her own separate income tax returns and will pay his or her individual income taxes from the funds available to the parties as they are earned, whether joint or separate, with no right of reimbursement to the other for the payment of either party's taxes.

All property or household goods purchased from the date when the partners began living together as defined in this agreement shall be owned jointly by the partners, as shall other assets and monies as defined herein. Any dispute as to ownership shall be resolved by referring to the date of purchase or acquisition of same.

Any banking accounts and funds, which are to remain as the separate property of either partner, or real properties or other assets, are defined herein in the attached schedules, and shall remain as the separate property of the party owning same pursuant to this agreement, together with any increases thereon, as defined herein, and shall be maintained by the respective parties free from commingling of such funds.

ARTICLE 6
PROPERTY AND LIABILITIES OF MARTINA

6.01 Property and Liabilities of MARTINA

The property described on Schedule A, attached to this agreement and made a part of it for all purposes, is and will remain the separate property of MARTINA.

The liabilities and obligations described on Schedule C, attached to this agreement and made a part of it for all purposes, are the sole liabilities and obligations of MARTINA, to be satisfied and paid solely from her separate estate and from which she will forever hold harmless, indemnify, and defend JUDY from any claim.

Any taxes, interest, or penalties that MARTINA may owe for income received or accrued by her or that are otherwise attributable to her are the sole liabilities and obligations of MARTINA, but can and shall be paid from the income which shall hereafter be jointly owned by the parties, save and except that she shall forever hold harmless, indemnify, and defend JUDY from any claims against her estate, free from reimbursement to JUDY for any taxes attributable to any separate estate which MARTINA may incur.

ARTICLE 7
PROPERTY AND LIABILITIES OF JUDY

7.01 Property and Liabilities of Judy

The property described on Schedule B, attached to this agreement and made a part of it for all purposes, is and will remain the separate property of JUDY.

The liabilities and obligations described on Schedule D, attached to this agreement and made a part of it for all purposes, are the sole liabilities and obligations of JUDY, to be satisfied and paid solely from her separate estate and from which she will forever hold harmless, indemnify, and defend MARTINA from any claim, save and except that she shall have the right should she so desire to use the funds earned jointly by the parties to pay any such liabilities and obligations without claim from the other partner for a reimbursement for same.

Any taxes, interest, or penalties that JUDY may owe for income received or accrued by her or that are otherwise attributable to her are the sole liabilities and obligations of JUDY, but can and shall be paid from the income which shall hereafter be jointly owned by the parties, save and except that she shall forever hold harmless, indemnify, and defend MARTINA from any claims against her estate, and shall further not be obligated to reimburse MARTINA for any sums so incurred as a result of her separate estate.

ARTICLE 8
FUTURE CREDIT TRANSACTIONS

8.01 Future Credit Transactions of Parties

Recognizing the complexity of modern business credit transactions and because each partner desires to allow the other to enter into such transactions without the other's approval or joinder or nonjoinder, the parties make the following agreement respecting such future credit transactions. If either partner enters into a transaction wherein credit is extended to that partner or that partner becomes liable or obligated for the repayment, contingent or otherwise, of credit extended to any third party, whether or not the transaction is appropriately denominated as a "separate-property" transaction, and unless a contrary intent is specifically and expressly stated, then that obligation will be satisfied by the partner incurring it from the joint funds earned by the parties without claim for reimbursement from the other for such credit extended or paid. The assets, if any, acquired through any such credit transaction will be and remain the joint property of the partners regardless of which partner purchased same, but such party incurring the liability shall hold harmless the other's estate for such liability.

Should any business failure occur subsequent to the commencement of the agreement by the partners hereto, for any business which shall be determined to be the joint business of the parties as defined herein because same was acquired after the commencement of the agreement, or any bankruptcy, reorganization, composition, arrangement, or other debtor/creditor action of or against the partners will look to each other jointly for any credit, accommodation, or indulgence in this regard. Similarly, should any business failure occur in connection with a business owned by either partner as their separate property because same was acquired prior to the commencement of this agreement, then such loss shall be paid from the separate property of the partner having incurred such loss from their separate estate.

ARTICLE 9
MANAGEMENT, DISPOSITION, AND
TRANSMUTATION OF PROPERTY

9.01 Management of Properties

Each partner will have the full, free, and unrestricted right to manage his or her separate property, including, without limitation, the right to convey or encumber that property; to dispose of it by sale, gift, or otherwise; and to deal with it without taking into consideration the other partner.

9.02 Disposition of Property of the Other Person

Notwithstanding any other provision of this agreement, either partner may, only by appropriate, notarized written instrument, transfer, give, convey, devise, or bequeath any property defined herein as the separate property of that partner to the other. Neither partner intends by this agreement to limit or restrict in any way the right to receive any such transfer, gift, conveyance, devise, or bequest from the other, except as stated in this agreement.

ARTICLE 10
GENERAL PROVISIONS

10.01 Separation, Definition, and Division of Assets

The parties have heretofore agreed that a separation may occur at the request of either party and shall be officially denied as that period when either party notifies the other in writing that they so desire for a separation to occur.

In that event, each party shall make a complete list, to the best of their ability of all of the assets and monies on hand, separating those lists into three categories:

List 1 shall define all of MARTINA's separate property and monies;

List 1A shall define all of the items which MARTINA alleges are gifts to her and shall further enumerate when such gifts were acquired, and from whom they were given, and for what occasion.

List 2 shall define all of JUDY's separate property and monies;

List 2A shall define all of the items which JUDY alleges are gifts to her, and shall further enumerate when such gifts were acquired, and from whom they were given, and for what occasion.

List 3 shall determine all of the property and monies acquired since the date of the commencement of this agreement, save and except for the gifts enumerated in Lists 1A and 2A respectively cited hereinabove.

It is the intent of this agreement to award all of MARTINA's separate property, as defined herein, and which should comprise List 1 and List 1A to her; to award all of JUDY's separate property, as defined herein, and which should comprise List 2 and 2A to her; and to divide all of the items, monies, properties, etc. remaining, which shall be all of those items, monies, etc. acquired since the commencement of this agreement, and which are still on hand equally to the parties.

In this regard, each party shall prepare a list detailing what they would consider to be a fair division or exchange of assets in an attempt to reach an equal division of the assets remaining on hand for division. In the event there are any assets remaining that the parties cannot agree upon the division of or to whom same should be awarded, such assets shall be sold and the proceeds equally divided. Either party may buy or sell any asset to the other by written agreement.

In the event there is real estate involved, and like assets cannot be exchanged, or a buy/sell agreement cannot be made for same, the item of real estate shall be placed upon the market for sale and the proceeds equally divided. The parties may each equally continue to use and enjoy any real estate so involved, and shall share equally in any payments and upkeep after separation and pending the sale of same. In the event that either party defaults on such payments or upkeep after separation and pending sale of same, and the other party expends monies in excess of the defaulting party, such paying party shall be reimbursed from the defaulting parties' share of the proceeds of such real estate upon the sale of same for the difference in monies expended after separation.

Immediately subsequent to any separation, and prior to any division of the assets, monies, etc. herein defined as the joint property of the parties, both parties shall refrain from spending or disposing of assets, monies, or any other property which may be construed to be the joint property of the parties pending a division of same. In the event either party shall have expended or otherwise disposed of property which is later determined to be the joint property of the parties, that party shall reimburse the other party for one half of such sums or properties which she disposed of from her share of the division of the remaining estate.

AGREEMENT/MARTINA NAVRATILOVA – JUDY NELSON

ARTICLE 11
GENERAL PROVISIONS

11.01   Benefit and Burden

This agreement will be binding on and inure to
the benefit of the partners and their respective heirs,
administrators, personal representatives, successors, and
assigns.

11.02   Consideration for Agreement

The consideration for this agreement is the mutual
promise of each partner to act as companion and homemaker
to the other, in addition to the other specific promises
contained in this agreement. Any services that either partner
may provide to the other or for the benefit of the other are
fully compensated by this agreement.

11.03   Fiduciary Duty

Each partner promises to act in good faith and to deal
fairly with the other in the management of their joint
property in acting under the terms of this agreement.

11.04   Support After Separation or Death

Each partner waives the right to be supported by the
other after their separation or after the death of either
partner, and each partner agrees not to make any claim for
such support.

11.05   No Intention to Create "Common-Law" or "Informal"
Marriage

Neither party will hold himself out as the other party's
spouse. The partners are not married at the effective date of
this agreement, and do not intend to marry at some future
date. Neither partner intends to or will do any act or cause
any result that will create a factual situation that would create
a "common-law marriage" or a presumption in favor of such
relationship, an "informal marriage" as defined in

AGREEMENT/MARTINA NAVRATILOVA – JUDY NELSON

sections 1.91 and 1.92 of the Texas Family Code and any cases construing those statutes, or any other public reputation of living together as husband and wife. Any subsequent marriage between the partners must therefore be a formal ceremonial marriage, and any such marriage will affect this agreement only as provided in paragraph 2.01 above.

11.06 Integration

This agreement sets forth the entire agreement between the partners with regard to the subject matter of the agreement. All agreements, covenants, representations, and warranties, express and implied, oral and written, of the partners concerning their financial relationship, past, present, and future, commencing as of the date they began living together and terminating if and when they separate, are contained in this agreement. No other agreements, covenants, representations, or warranties, express or implied, oral or written, have been made by either partner to the other regarding the subject matter of this agreement. All prior and contemporaneous conversations, negotiations, possible and alleged agreements and representations, covenants, and warranties regarding the subject matter of this agreement are waived, merged in this agreement, and superseded by this agreement. This is an integrated agreement.

11.07 Severability

If any provision of this agreement is deemed to be invalid or unenforceable, it shall be deemed severable from the remainder of the agreement, which will continue in full force and effect without being impaired or invalidated in any way. If a provision is deemed invalid because of its scope or breadth, it shall be deemed valid to the extent of the scope or breadth permitted by law.

11.08 Amendment

This agreement can be amended only by a written agreement signed by both partners in the presence of a notary public.

AGREEMENT/MARTINA NAVRATILOVA – JUDY NELSON

11.09 Governing Law

All rights, duties, and obligations under this agreement are payable and enforceable in Fort Worth, Tarrant County, Texas. This agreement shall be governed by, and construed and enforced in accordance with, the laws of the state of Texas.

11.10 Signing of Agreement

Prior to the execution of this agreement, each partner was clearly warned that they should individually consult with an attorney of her own choice, and further defined and have clearly explained all of the many terms and legal significance of the agreement and the effect it has on any interest that either partner might accrue in the property of the other were fully explained. Each partner acknowledges that she understands and that she fully understands the agreement and its legal effect, that she is signing the agreement freely and voluntarily, and that neither partner has any reason to believe that the other did not fully understand the terms and effects of the agreement or that she did not freely and voluntarily execute the agreement, and that each individually waived the right to have an attorney and that each desired to sign same without consultation or the involvement of an attorney.

Each partner further acknowledged that they had jointly and mutually determined what they wanted their partnership to involve and what they intended for their respective property rights to be, and they each agreed that they desired to have those rights reduced to a written agreement which they had pre-determined the contents of. They further acknowledged that they understood and consequences and benefits of this agreement and each individually requested that they have no outside interference or assistance from an attorney or any other person, and further contracted and agreed that the determination to waive their individual rights to separate counsel is not and shall never become an issue to set aside or in any manner contest any provision of this contract in a court of law or any other forum.

11.11 Interpretation

No provision in this agreement is to be interpreted for or against any partner because that partner or that partner's legal representative drafted the provision.

11.12 Costs and Expenses

Each partner will bear her own costs and expenses incurred in connection with this agreement, including, without limitation, its negotiation, preparation, and consummation.

11.13 Attorney's Fees

If any partner retains counsel for the purpose of enforcing or preventing the breach of any provision of this agreement, including, but not limited to, by instituting any action or proceeding to enforce any provision of the agreement, for damage by reason of any alleged breach of any provision of the agreement, for a declaration of that partner's rights or obligations under the agreement, or for any other judicial remedy, then the prevailing partner will be entitled to be reimbursed by the losing partner for all costs and expenses incurred thereby, including, but not limited to, reasonable attorney's fees and costs for the services rendered to the prevailing partner.

EXECUTED in multiple originals on the date of the acknowledgments shown below.

Witness

Witness

MARTINA NAVRATILOVA
Partner

Witness

Witness

JUDY NELSON
Partner

STATE OF TEXAS

COUNTY OF ____Tarrant____

This instrument was acknowledged before me on February 27, 1986, by MARTINA NAVRATILOVA.

[seal]

_____

Notary Public, State of Texas
Commission Expires:_____
Typed or Printed Name of
Notary

_____

STATE OF TEXAS

COUNTY OF ____Tarrant____

This instrument was acknowledged before me on February 27, 1986, by JUDY NELSON.

[seal]

_____

Notary Public, State of Texas
Commission Expires: _____
Typed or Printed Name of
Notary

_____

Acceptance:
Martina Is Gone for Good

On February 4, 1991, only days after Martina left the Star-wood house, Bales, eighteen, and Eddie, twenty, both faxed independent, heartfelt letters to Martina at the ranch. The boys felt a tremendous sense of loss without Martina, but that was overshadowed by their deep concern for their mother. Judy was depressed and despondent, unable to pull herself together without help from her family. As usual, she spoke to them almost daily, but the most they could do was to listen to her and comfort her.

The letters from the boys to Martina speak for themselves:

Martina,

I don't really know what to say, but I will do my best. I think you should know that we all think of you as part of our family and we will go to the farthest extremes to make things work.

I have been through this situation before and I know it's no "walk in the park." We must all pull together and function as one strong family. No matter how distant we all seem, we still have to be strong. I know mom loves you and I love you with all my heart. I know, with time on our side, that the sun will shine again and all our problems will be solved. Just know that you have had one of the biggest influences on me. The respect that I have for you and mom goes beyond imagination. Together the two of you create a team that could never be defeated.

Understand that I can't possibly understand the magnitude of the situation. In my 17 years I have seen my parents divorce but I also saw them fight. No matter how hard they fought, they just couldn't make it work. But they tried. You and mom must try! You need each other, and if you search your deepest emotions, you will see that this is the truth.

I take no side in the situation because I am here as a support to the two most important people in my life. Martina, I want you to be with me and my family until death does us part. You have not only served as an idol, teacher, and friend but you also have taken on a role of a "parentlike figure" in my life. I love you as if you were my mom and I always know that you will be there for me.

You are the greatest.

I Love you,
Bales

Eddie made a similar attempt to communicate with Martina from Fort Worth:

Dear Martina,

I just want you to know that I love you very much. You have meant so much to me over the years as an inspiration, a motivator, and a great friend. You are part of my family and losing a family member is a heart-breaking blow; especially one as dear and valuable as yourself.

I am well aware that I can not fathom all that goes on right now. I cannot possibly feel what you feel. I do know, however, that emotions are powerful, and I can only hope that you don't allow your emotions to cloud your ability to contemplate your past and weigh that past against your future. Mom gave her life, her heart to you many years ago, and continues to give today.

Such knowledge pervades my every thought. I hurt for her more now than when my father left because I know the scope of her love for you, a love that never dies. You must know that such devotion and care are so very rare in this world.

Regardless of the outcome, I know your actions will be the right ones for you. I believe in you. I believe I am the luckiest person in the world for having you in my life.

Because of you, my life has become all the better. Don't go away.

Eddie

Several days later, Martina responded to Bales's letter, with a fax promising him she would call and talk to him. However, she didn't talk to either of the boys until September, when she saw them in court.

By March, Martina had moved on, but needed to negotiate with Judy a fair division of the real estate acquired during their time together, which now included three properties in Aspen: the Ranch, the Starwood House, and the small house near Independence Pass. During a telephone conversation with Judy in Aspen, Martina finally asked her the inevitable but uncomfortable question: "What is it that you want?"

"I want what was in the agreement," Judy replied evenly but firmly, trying to leave no doubt about her resolve.

Judy believed Martina was now forced to face the consequences of what she had allegedly promised to Judy five years earlier in their partnership agreement.

Although she may have hoped that Judy would settle for less, Martina wrote Judy a letter which complied with the terms outlined in the agreement for terminating the partnership. As per the agreement, she informed Judy "in writing" that she wished to end the agreement. Martina did just that in a letter to Judy in March 1991. It appears that Martina was covering her bases while trying to exit with dignity, Martina added that she didn't think the document was binding. She closed the letter to Judy with "Sorry, Martina."

With Martina's letter in her hand, the seriousness of the situation became even more apparent to Judy—the emotional challenges were now compounded by legal ones. As Judy was struggling with her feelings about losing Martina, she was now forced to fight with her.

People who several months earlier had been part of Judy's life were now staunchly against her, siding with Martina. When Judy was living with Martina, these people gave her the same respect they would show a spouse. Now, however, the game had changed, the line had been drawn, and never again would she be allowed back into the circle.

According to Judy, when Martina was first confronted with the 1986 cohabitation agreement, she stated casually that she barely remembered signing it and then asked Judy to produce an original. Judy panicked when she realized she couldn't remember what had become of her copy. She vainly searched her files, and, for two days, she feared she was doomed—no document, no case. Then she remembered that the document had been locked in the safe at the Starwood house, but the combination was written on a closet wall in the Fort Worth home. Judy's former secretary in that city had to drive over to the Roaring Springs house, find the combination, then fax Judy in Aspen, who rushed to the downstairs closet and dialed the code. When the safe opened, she went directly to the document, pulled it out, and sighed with relief.

At this point, according to Judy, Peter Johnson, Martina's manager from International Management Group telephoned her and asked her to set aside the document and settle with Martina quickly, while Judy still had money to live on. At this point, without her knowledge, all credit cards, car and health insurance, and access to checking and saving accounts had been stripped away. That process had actually been set into effect by Martina's instructions, just a day after Martina left Judy in February. IMG flatly froze all of Judy's accounts and revoked all privileges. This was sticky business, since IMG had represented Judy since 1988 by providing tax and estate planning, while maintaining Judy's personal and business bank accounts and rendering investment advice with respect to her pension and profit-sharing plans. It appeared as though IMG was willfully interfering with a contract made between two of their own clients. If true, they had a conflict-of-interest problem.

Judy interpreted Peter Johnson's words to imply that she would have to leave the Sherwood house during the litigation process. Moreover, it would be in her best interest to settle out of court to avoid an ugly, protracted legal skirmish. He reminded her that Martina and IMG had the important financial and emotional weapons with which she might be destroyed and that she had better give in immediately, if she wished to keep any part of her private life out of the public eye.

Judy responded that the offer on the table at that time was simply not acceptable and that she was going to hold fast to her position. What was unspoken was the fact that Judy took Peter Johnson at his word and decided, by the direction of the conversation and the tone he had used over the phone, that she better dig in her heels and fight like hell for what she believed was fair. Martina and IMG had clearly underestimated her personal resolve and patience. The very qualities that had attracted Martina to Judy initially were the very ones she now found intolerable. Martina was clearly willing to go to the mat with Judy to break her spirit. For Judy, the issue was not only financial, but a matter of dignity and equality. It was about honoring your word— keeping a promise. She reasoned: why should more powerful people enjoy such an advantage in our American justice system? A celebrity should be held accountable for agreements and contracts; no one should be allowed to walk away from responsibility simply because he or she is a sports hero or because there might be pressure and prejudice involving a same-sex couple. As Judy put it, "In my eyes, the lawyers and the legal system should work the same for all people. A contract is a contract. If you sign it, you should be responsible for it."

Judy realized that in the months ahead, after Martina and IMG were finished designing and implementing a public campaign against her, the public would likely perceive her as greedy and self-serving. Her only hope of winning would be to show a jury that things are not always as they appear. She had no idea what it would take to persuade a jury—or the public at large— that things in the Navratilova camp were not always as they seemed. She did know people were not going to take her word for it that these credible professionals had gotten ugly, and she was certain that these professionals would leave no traces, no damaging paper trails.

Martina called Judy shortly after her "Dear Jane" letter, and

Judy recorded the call without informing Martina ahead of time. Judy said that she had the tape recorder on the phone in the first place because she had received some obscene phone calls. A suggestion was made that she try to record one of these conversations, as she thought she recognized the voice. Martina was a secondary thought but, in retrospect, Judy was glad that she had the recorder in place for a couple of their conversations. During this particular conversation, Martina was calm and sounded somewhat hopeful about the possibility of an out-of-court settlement. Judy's voice was fragile, and Martina seemed somewhat responsive to her vulnerability, but obviously wanted to get on with business. The subsequent conversation makes one point perfectly clear: Martina had no doubts about her new direction and Judy needed to accept that reality—immediately.

Judy: "Okay. So you want me to call Jerry, and I need to get him with your attorney?"

Martina: "Yeah, to call him and get to meet because he is not, you know, returning calls at all."

Judy: "Well, that's because I told him he wasn't going to do it."

Martina: "I know. He could do that. He could say no, we're not supposed to meet, but he didn't do it; but it doesn't matter. Just let them get together and try to work something out without——It doesn't mean we are going to court. It just means that they are trying to work it out."

Judy: "So do we hire lawyers?"

Martina: "Well, we already have done that."

Judy: "Well, no, I don't owe Jerry a cent, you know; and I am trying not to have to pay him a cent. But, you know, if that's what you want to do, then, you know, then I will hire the lawyer to do that."

Martina: "Well, doing that—I mean, he wanted to meet."

Judy: "Oh, I know that, he wanted to help me, you know. Sure."

Martina: "Well, he can—"

Judy: "But, he wasn't, you know, he is not charging me anything unless I tell him, okay, you know, that this is—I am going to have to have you."

Martina: "Well you have had him, you know. I don't
see——"

Judy: "Well, up till now, he's just been a friend; and he
has just tried to help me, you know, that this is—I
am going to have to have you."

Martina: "No, if you don't think so [inaudible], just pay him
by the hour."

Judy: "Well, I haven't even sat down to talk to him about
these things with him. I'll have to do that."

Martina: "Well, that's what I am asking."

Judy: "What are you asking me?"

Martina: "To pay him by the hour, not a percentage of what
you are going to get."

Judy: "Well, I have that choice."

Martina: "Yeah, of course you have a choice."

Judy: "Well, Martina, I don't know. I have never been
through this before."

Martina: "Of course, you have a choice. Percentages, you
know, then you are—I guess safe because if you
don't get anything, you don't owe him anything.
But, you know if you get—usually they take thirty
to forty percent and I don't know—I don't know if
he thinks what kind of chance he has to win, if it
goes that far or how much."

Judy: "What is—"

Martina: "He's better off taking—But I think for you, you
should pay him by the hour."

Judy: "I . . . thirty . . . between thirty and forty percent if
there is a settlement, or else just paid by the hour,
you hire them on a commission. I mean just a
straight-out fee . . . Yeah."

Martina: "If I have to pay the money, I'd rather give it to
you than the lawyer."

Judy: "Yeah. Well, that's why I was hoping we could do
it ourselves."

Martina: "Well, we can. We tried, but . . ."

Judy: "I try."

Martina: "You know your accountant, if that's who it is, or
your lawyer is telling you one thing and mine is
telling me another."

Judy: "Yeah."

Martina: "So we are trying to meet in the middle."

Judy: "Yeah. Well, however you want it, that's what I will do."

Martina: "Okay. They're telling me I think my guy was available this week, so I want to do it pretty quickly."

Judy: "Okay."

Martina: "Okay."

Judy: "Yeah. However you want it."

Martina: "Workable."

Judy: "Okay."

Martina: "It's not how I wanted it, but it needs to be done. I will talk to you later. Are you okay? Judy?"

At this point in the conversation, Judy begins to cry. Martina was on top of business and kept asserting that she wanted to get on with her life. Judy was helpless against Martina's clarity; she was just beginning her grieving process. The tape continues:

Judy: "Yeah, I'm okay."

Martina: "I want everything to work out so we will be friends, put this behind us as fast as possible."

Judy: "Me, too. I will. Tell Craig I said hi."

Martina: "I will."

Judy: "Bye-bye."

Martina: "Bye-bye."

Judy hung up the phone and quietly and slowly walked around the kitchen, her knees weak from the emotional drain she experienced while talking to Martina. She stared at the tape recorder for a moment, looking through the small window where the tape lay nestled in the machine, and then she pushed the rewind button, watching the tape as it rewound itself. She felt hopeless. She now had documentation of her worst fear as she stood and stared at the recorder. She wondered, "Where has she gone? That person I adored . . . that person I would have done anything for . . . that person who couldn't stand being separated from me for even a few days—where has she gone?"

Judy recalled that she dared herself to play the tape again. She reached for the play button, which she saw through watery eyes and, as she hit the button, her eyes brimmed over, and she sobbed as she listened to Martina's voice, her clarity, her distance.

Martina was holding firmly to her position: she hadn't read the contract and wasn't about to honor it. Judy filed a petition with the court charging her with breach of contract and, just two days before Martina left for Europe to play Eastbourn and Wimbledon, she was served with a notice to appear. After practice one afternoon, Martina walked over to someone beckoning her as she was leaving. Thinking at first she was being asked to sign an autograph for someone she thought was a fan, she saw the legal documents that awaited her signature. Martina was enraged. Judy had distracted her before Wimbledon. Judy, of all people, aware of how important it was for her to give her undivided attention to her task of winning one more Wimbledon. By the next day, the press had already picked up on the news and were running excerpts from the video of the signing of the agreement because it had been admitted as evidence when Judy filed the lawsuit.

Knowing that she would be headed for court and that the tape would be entered into evidence, Martina granted an interview to *A Current Affair* television show. On the air, she stated that she was disappointed and that she and Judy had had a good relationship, and added that she couldn't believe it all came down to greed.

During Wimbledon, NBC aired a twelve-minute segment with Judy in Fort Worth with interviewer Gail Gardner. Judy appeared tearful and said that she wished she could have accompanied Martina at Wimbledon, and that she was lonely without her. NBC joined this footage with footage of Martina's winning moment just one year earlier, when she jumped into her player's box, and embraced everyone sitting there: Ma, Bigs, Bales and his friend Dru, Craig, Billie Jean, and Judy. The contrast was startling.

Later, on the court at Wimbledon, Martina was upset by fifteen-year-old Jennifer Capriati, 6–4, 7–5, in the quarterfinals: her earliest dismissal from the tournament in over a decade. It would be recorded on TV interviews that Billie Jean, Chris Evert, and Tracy Austin did not feel that the public controversy between the two women would account for any losses, but in Martina's case the distraction would serve as a catapult for complete focus. Then, as was usually the scenario with Martina, the tennis court would become her sanctuary—an escape from the worldly situations. Some thought differently.

When Martina returned home, she granted Barbara Walters an interview which aired on *20/20* in late July and helped the show gain its highest rating ever. This was unfortunate for Judy, since Martina kept assaulting her character and the millions of viewers heard only one side. Why didn't Barbara Walters also air Judy's side? ABC never asked for an interview with Judy and never pretended to give a balanced account, stating at the beginning of the program that Judy had said her piece during Wimbledon.

Hugh Downs opened with the teaser: "The tangled, fascinating, now turbulent life of one of the most accomplished athletes in history. Name almost any record in tennis, and next to it you'll likely find the name Martina Navratilova. From the game's rookie of the year in 1974 to athlete of the decade for the eighties, Martina Navratilova has dominated her chosen sport in a way that few athletes ever have.

"But now she's center court in a different situation; a lawsuit by a former woman companion. Martina hasn't been interviewed on the subject until this week, when she agreed to talk exclusively to Barbara.

"Martina says that as she faces that lawsuit, she has less money than people think. She cites bad tax advice and says she lived very high, supporting herself and her lover, Judy Nelson, and her family. Earlier in the month, as Martina was trying to win her tenth Wimbledon title, Nelson served her with a summons. Then, as part of their Wimbledon coverage, NBC broadcast an interview with Judy Nelson. She detailed her intimate relationship with Navratilova and gave the reasons for her lawsuit. So, as part of our agreement with Martina, is that since Judy gave her side on television, this would be Martina's turn."

"Today she faces perhaps the greatest challenge in a lifetime of challenges . . ." After a brief biographical section, Walters cut to the chase: "What raised eyebrows, though, was her life off the court. . . . women. In 1984, with her tennis career well in stride, Martina fell in love with a Texas beauty queen ten years her senior. Onetime model, a former Cotton Maid, the wife of a successful doctor, mother of two sons, Judy left the marriage and the children to move in with Martina." At this point, tabloid papers from 1984 appear on the screen. "Texas Beauty Is New Gal Pal in Martina's Life." Walters continues, as images from the London tabloids flash quickly by. "She became a main feature at courtside and the mainstay of what Martina herself would call 'Team Navratilova.' She was the principal fan for Martina's ninth singles victory last year at Wimbledon.

"But earlier this year they broke up. And the focus of their relationship moved from the tennis court to the courthouse. Judy Nelson sued Martina in Texas, where they had lived, for fifty percent of her property earnings. The lawsuit is based on a document, signed by both before a video camera five years ago."

Excerpts of the video, that both had hoped would remain private, rolled across the screen. This particular *20/20* was the most watched broadcast in over a decade. Finally, Walters appeared with Navratilova.

"Well," Walters begins, "let's get to those questions everyone asks and wants to have answered." Martina's eyebrows rise a bit, then she smiles and listens attentively, knowing what is about to be asked. "You sat with Judy Nelson in 1986, that was just two years after your relationship began, and you taped an agreement in which you would split fifty-fifty any money that either of you made. Why did you agree to this?"

"Because I didn't know that is exactly what it meant. I would have no reason to do something like that, other than to give everything away that I have worked for. Here I am now, I've been playing tennis for now eighteen years, and I've been working really hard. Why would I be willing to give half of that to someone who really had nothing to do with my tennis career?"

Barbara jumps in. "But you *signed* it. You're not dumb, Martina, you're a smart lady. What did you think you were signing; what did you think you were agreeing to?"

"I thought I was paying Judy a certain amount of money for every year we were together. And if we should split up, then that is what she should get. I never thought we would split. I thought that was the relationship that was going to last the rest of my life, but I still didn't think I would be giving away half of what I made. I thought the half was if Judy and I ever got into a business together, I would get half and Judy would get half. That is fair, fair enough. And as actually happened with the clothing company—we started a clothing business—and Judy got half and I got half. I thought that was logical. But certainly not if I go out and win a tournament and make $100,000 that $50,000 of that should go to Judy.

"So you thought if it was a *new* business, fine, but not that she should get fifty percent of your tennis," said Walters.

"Not of the money I made on the tennis court. She had nothing to do with that. I'm the one that's hitting the tennis ball out there," Martina replied.

"Well, when you see the tape—we've seen it, a lot of people have—you looked as if you were uncomfortable, but also seemed as if you understood what it was you were being asked to do . . ."

They show the beginning of the tape. After a short segment, Martina says, "You see, as this—this is the first time I'm hearing this as she is saying it on the tape. When I signed and initialed all the pages, I hadn't read them. What I thought I was signing was essentially that agreement, which was one of the pages of handwritten notes, both mine and Judy's handwriting, and out of that we got eleven pages of typed notes, so I should have gotten a clue right then and there. And as BeAnn is talking and saying these things, I'm thinking to myself, 'This is not what I thought it was,' but I didn't want to make waves. I figured Judy wouldn't try to do something backhanded like that. I trusted her and I trusted the lawyers, and now I'm in big trouble."

"Do you think it was premeditated, that Judy realized what she was doing at the time?" Walters asked.

"I have to believe that she really and truly loved me, but I also now believe that this was pretty much organized ahead of time. She figured either she was going to have me or have a lot of money because otherwise there would have been no reason to write something up like this. And when we did break up, Judy said, 'Well, there is this agreement; you have to pay me half.' And I didn't know what she was talking about. I totally forgot about it. In the video. And the video, the reason for doing the video in the first place was, I thought, to protect my parents, because with the agreement was also a will, where my parents get half and Judy gets half. I wanted to protect Judy from my parents, which is a joke now."

Walters interjects, "You mean so your parents wouldn't claim everything?"

"Exactly."

"This is not a legal relationship—Judy gets nothing?"

"Yeah, that was the purpose of the video. As it turns out, I was helping Judy and hurting myself by doing that."

"Did you try to settle?"

"Yes, absolutely. Her lawyer would not meet with my lawyer, he said, unless we were willing to talk about three million dollars. I didn't have that kind of money."

"There are rumors that you offered her two million. Is that right?"

"No, I did not. I don't have that kind of money. If I give her that, I'm broke. I may as well start all over again, eighteen years of playing tennis down the drain."

"How do you feel about her now, this woman you loved?"

"Totally betrayed. My failure is that I don't love her anymore. Well, should you pay for that?"

"Your lawyers are implying that this actually is a 'signed contract.' You had a sexual relationship with Judy, and this is what it is."

"Well, obviously, the only reason why there was any agreement was because we had a relationship. We lived as man and wife: two women living together, loving each other."

"Do you consider this agreement 'sex for money'?"

"No, I wouldn't go that far. Love for money, maybe."

"Homosexuality is illegal in Texas, where this agreement was signed. What does that do to your agreement?"

"Well, even the lawyers who drew it up said they 'were not sure if this is legal, but we're doing it anyway.' That would seem to make it illegal. But that's up to the lawyers. God knows how those cases go."

"Do you know that Judy Nelson said that she did handle everything for your traveling, your clothes, your food? I quote: 'I did everything for Martina but hit the tennis ball.' "

"Yeah, well, I had been doing pretty well before I met Judy. I had managed things on my own, and I am managing well now."

"When you were together, did you give Judy a salary?"

"Yeah, starting in 1985, a year after we began living together, and all the way through to 1990, she was paid $90,000 a year."

"$90,000 a year?"

"Yes, so whatever she did she was paid for."

Barbara and Martina talked about Martina's relationship with Nancy Lieberman, then got back to Judy.

"Judy left her husband and two sons, gave up custody of her sons. She left what was considered a normal heterosexual relationship for you. Do you feel responsible for that?"

"No. I did not pursue Judy. I told her I don't want to be responsible for that. When she told me after six or eight weeks since we began having a relationship that she was going to leave her husband and kids, I panicked. Because I felt responsible; it was my doing. She said absolutely not. She was going to leave anyway. I just speeded it up. They were having problems in their marriage anyway. I just gave her a reason to leave."

"Why did the relationship with Judy break up after seven years? Last year after you won Wimbledon, the first thing you did was look in the stands and saw her. You were obviously very close."

"Yes, we were very close. I don't want to get into too many personal things here, but we were having problems for the last couple of years, and shortly after New Year's we started having deeper discussions about it. Judy knew there were problems. It hurt as though I just got up and left—said 'see you later' . . . There was just no future in that relationship for me anymore."

"What has been the worst part of this entire ordeal?"

"I think it's the personal trust that has gone into the wind. I've always been one who trusted people until proven otherwise. Now the person I trusted with my life, who I felt for sure was not in it for the money has proven me wrong. . . ."

Now that Judy was no longer Martina's companion, her sexual preference was no longer a simple matter of having chosen to be with a woman. Had this relationship been a fluke? Would she go "back to men"? People kept asking these questions, but it was far too soon for Judy to focus on romance or to even entertain the idea of trusting again. Emotionally, she still hadn't let go of her relationship with Martina, doomed as it certainly appeared to everyone else who knew the situation. Unrealistic as it might have been, she still imagined a reunion, a return to the life they had built and shared together.

Throughout the early months of 1991, Judy had been turning to her family and friends in Aspen and Fort Worth to help her through this difficult transition in her life. Yet eventually the comfort they offered her was not enough; she felt she needed an expert to guide her through her grief. Judy sought help from a friend and therapist named Annie Denver, John Denver's former wife and the inspiration for his hit, "Annie's Song." She was sensitive to Judy's need to recover and grow from this experience and was able to add an element of compassion that comes only from shared experience.

May 1991 marked the beginning of a year of painfully unstable moods, marked by extreme highs and lows, which Judy experienced on her way to self-realization and self-reliance. This was a strengthening period that would lead her to search her own behavior and examine the motives in her relationship with Martina.

As she and Annie worked together in Aspen, Judy continued to move from a place of self-doubt toward a more settling sense of independence and "self," in the richest sense of the word. It's a powerful feeling of contentment that comes only from knowing that your relationship is with yourself and your world, rather than allowing yourself to be defined by the company you keep.

When you place someone—anyone—on a pedestal and spend your life supporting that person, he or she will eventually step down off the pedestal and walk. Count on it. It's structural, not personal, not gender specific. It's just that society does not value the caretaker, the one who lightens the load and clears the path. This is unfortunate, and it may change, but probably not in our lifetime. Judy was learning that the best way to take care of someone else was to take care of herself.

As Judy moved along the rough road of her emotional journey, she was forced to look at her caretaking role. It was time for reflection and self-exploration. She thought she had failed at both her traditional and alternative marriage, and while Ed Nelson and Martina shared responsibility for mistakes that were made, Judy needed to examine her role in their breakups.

With Martina, for example, perhaps she was too controlling, but Martina seemed to have needed something like that. Her emotional demands were not necessarily complex, but they were endless. She was an institution, of sorts, needing care for her body, her game, and her financial affairs while wanting to be pampered and encouraged when at home.

While all this was true, Judy still needed to examine what she gained out of having that kind of power and influence over someone. No doubt, control was an important issue. Judy had control over the situation, even when she didn't want it. Martina was busy training and playing, and she wasn't going to do the "dailies" and pay attention to boring details, especially not when someone else was eager to do them for her.

Judy had learned strength from her mother, and she labeled her behavior "responsible and supportive," but she didn't want this kind of control or responsibility for anyone else again. Controlling anything other than her own acts did not work. She lost herself in the other person—but if she was going to do that, why explore alternative lifestyles? Any woman can step into a caretaking role simply by following tradition. Judy was capable of more—and knew it.

Beyond psychological exploration, taking care of yourself during a particular personal crisis should include an exercise program. Judy herself poured it on, taking up tennis again (which, ironically, she had given up once she met Martina), and worked with her friend and trainer at the Aspen Club, Jim Landis, several times a week. This achieved two important things: it built muscle and gave her a routine. She needed the distraction and welcomed the muscles. The tabloids were suggesting that Martina had left an aging beauty queen who was over the hill. "Like hell" Judy thought as she pumped iron with a vengeance and flexed her muscles in the mirror.

It was during this time that Judy met and became friendly with Sandra Faulkner, a sociologist who lived in San Francisco. Sandra was vacationing in Aspen when they ran into each other while working out at the Aspen Club. Over lunch they discussed Judy's case. Sandra explained that she worked as a jury behavioral consultant, and they quickly engaged in a conversation about the voir dire process of interviewing potential jurors. It was impossible for Judy to talk about the case without discussing her feelings about Martina. As she spoke, tears flowed. She explained, "I hope we can settle out of court. I don't want to hurt her." She then added, "You do understand that, don't you?" What began as simple conversation about jury behavior became a heartfelt conversation about love and loss.

After Sandra returned to San Francisco, they continued to talk over the phone for the next two weeks. Judy invited her to return to Aspen, where she officially asked for help with jury selection, should the case fail to be resolved through negotiation.

It was now late May, and Judy had spent the winter and spring in her Starwood home alone, except for her two Persian cats. She had her telephone lines, and her friends in town, but it was time for a change of environment, time to do the things she had been unable to do because of Martina's touring schedule. Now that she would be home during the summer, she would be able to enjoy her horses, and her hiking at Crested Butte and could develop friendships in Aspen—things she and Martina had planned to do when they retired. She needed to keep the dreams they shared, to make them her own and realize them for herself. She had become accustomed to realizing many dreams, but she was accustomed to dreaming and sharing with Martina.

One antidote sprang to Judy's mind:—the St. James Club in Antigua, where Martina and she owned a villa that provided a vital haven every year after Wimbledon. Antigua was peaceful and warm and distant, a place where they could relax totally. Judy welcomed a change of scenery. The depression and loneliness would not subside. She gathered up five of her best girlfriends, two from Aspen and three from Texas, and headed for the villa, which was ideally located on a secluded island in the British West Indies, in an exclusive resort complex, surrounded by beaches lined with palm trees. The tennis pro and the diving instructor had been friends of Judy and Martina, often sharing meals and hosting parties.

The week Judy spent in Antigua with her friends brought about a crucial breakthrough and marked the moment that she knew she would make it in her life without Martina.

Prior to the trip, life seemed heavy; she felt the weight of sorrow upon her; she walked slowly and couldn't sleep. She would swing from a manic state of not sleeping all night to days when she could hardly move. All of her unexpressed anger had turned inward, creating depression. She would laugh, but it was hollow. She existed, but her days were meaningless. Yet, once she reached Antigua, a transformation began. Real laughter returned. The sun was a healing source of energy. Her friends were attentive and genuine. She finally began to get in touch with her repressed anger and to bring that poison to the surface. Once she could finally feel rage for being left with such disregard for her well-being, she could divest herself of blame. Letting go was its own reward, for Judy knew she had the courage, once again, to change her life; to put an end to the relationship that had meant the world to her for seven years and to structure the rest of her life primarily considering her own needs.

Eddie would enter graduate school in two years, Bales would go to college in a year, and she was free to design her life. At this point, age forty-five, she knew what she didn't want and was learning to ask for what she needed. While in Antigua, Judy saw a glimpse of her future and it left her still fragile but hopeful. It was a spiritual, inner-self kind of experience. It came through the talks and laughter with her friends. Up to that point, Judy was not sure that she could ever love again. She remembers that a new and close friend, Maryann Schiller, convinced her that she could. Maryann herself was having to deal with a breakup with her boyfriend of several years. The two girls connected on a highly emotional level, both rebounding from losses of persons they had loved. Judy realized that she was not alone in her pain.

It was a new beginning. She gained new energy and a sense of self that she liked. Judy hadn't forced the change, it just happened as she gently started letting go of the fear, with the help of her friends. She was just beginning to understand that Martina simply needed to go her way, just as she herself had in 1984, when she left Ed. Judy saw no need for Martina to annihilate her emotionally. Instead, she got in touch with her anger and was finally coming to terms with the fact that the relationship, as she had known it, was over.

Sometime after returning from Antigua to Aspen, she took an overnight hike to Crested Butte. "It was about a seven-hour hike on foot that takes one into the clouds and nestles one down into the mountain," Judy remembered. "When I crossed over the peak and gazed upon the vast array of wildflowers, I ran with open arms and plunged myself into the center of this secret garden. I had never felt such peace—such calm. It was a very spiritual moment, and I was again aware that this marked another point in my healing process. At last I was moving toward personal independence. My son, Eddie, and my friend, Maryann, were there with me, and I threw my arms around them and softly asked them to someday have my ashes scattered on this field of wildflowers. They promised. I cried. I had never felt richer, nor more at peace with myself than at that moment."

After returning to her home that evening, Judy thought to herself, "Just when you think you have experienced the most beautiful place in the world, you climb over the ridge, and you are greeted by something even more spectacular."

11

The Hearing

On Monday, September 9, 1991, Martina Navratilova arrived in a Fort Worth courtroom, just two days after losing in the U.S. Open finals to Monica Seles in New York. All out-of-court attempts to settle her legal dispute with Judy Nelson had failed, and now—apparently—the lawyers would take over.

A reluctant Martina was in court to testify on behalf of the motion she had filed to remove Jerry Loftin from representing Judy. Martina's grounds: Loftin had violated a rule called "conflict of interest" because he allegedly obtained information about Martina's financial assets while representing her in several minor legal transactions. Paramount to the motion were allegations by Navratilova that Jerry Loftin's own firm had participated in drafting the agreement in question. This matter needed to be resolved before Judy and Martina could proceed with a trial to settle their dispute about the viability of the cohabitation agreement they had signed in 1986.

In Forth Worth, Martina's large legal team consisted of several attorneys and their assistants. "There were so many of them," Jerry Loftin later observed, "that when the judge entered the courtroom and they all rose to their feet, they looked as though they were doing a dance."

Navratilova's chief counsel was a short, fiery man in his mid-forties named Michael McCurly. He was a local boy, born and raised in Texas, and he was well armed with Southern charm and down-home orneriness. His dark hair, slicked back tight to his head, was just a little too long and well oiled to be considered current or stylish by anyone's standards—but he did wear cowboy boots. Before the week was over, McCurly would offer a slice of Texas culture that could only be found in a Texas courtroom.

This was a state whose justice system gave birth to such colorful characters as star defense attorney Racehorse Haynes (who gained fame by persuading the members of juries that criminals were simply "citizens accused," often allowing them to walk) and Hanging Judge Roy Bean (who took the law into his own hands in the early days of Texas law). Justified or not, Texas justice has always been perceived as being larger than life—bringing to mind payoffs, politics, or violence. While these perceptions are mostly mythological, folklore is hard to debunk, and when these legendary figures, like Mr. Haynes himself, eventually became players in this case, one couldn't help but sit back and take notice. This was a case of the Western genre seducing reality.

Judy had arrived from Aspen two days earlier and was staying with her family at their home near the Fort Worth Boat Club. Sandra had come in from San Francisco to meet her parents and the boys, but primarily to observe the courtroom proceedings in anticipation of her future role as a trial-behavior consultant. In the event of an eventual Nelson/Navratilova trial, it would be her job to help identify the social and psychological factors in the case and to assist Judy's counsel with jury selection.

Driving to the courthouse that first morning, the two prepared for the day ahead. At this point, they had known each other for only a couple of months, but were comfortable with each other and were able to offer each other quiet support. They were about to face the battle of Judy's life and the professional challenge of Sandra's career, trying their best to cope with the public scrutiny and private challenges involved in the battle against Martina. They entered the courthouse at 9:00 A.M., accompanied by Judy's legal team of Jerry Loftin, Richard Orsinger and BeAnn Sisemore, the paralegal who had helped Judy and Martina prepare their now very public document, "the nonmarital cohabitation agreement," in February 1986. BeAnn would be one of Loftin's principal witnesses.

While the hearing itself was narrowly focused to resolve Jerry Loftin's ongoing legal status with Judy, the ramifications ran much deeper. How, in fact, could Martina's good ol' boy, Mc-Curly argue that Loftin should be removed from the case without discussing the validity of the 1986 agreement entered into freely by Judy and Martina? This entire episode would have to be examined, if only to serve a larger purpose, and to shape future strategy by both sides. Obviously the hearing would serve more as a backdrop for what had become a well-publicized contest between two lesbians over an agreement that gave one of them the privileges reserved for wives and the other the obligations traditionally shouldered by the husband. Place at the heart of this drama an international tennis star and a former Maid of Cotton fighting over an estate estimated at more than nine million dollars and one can easily understand why the press was assembled at the courthouse well before the litigants arrived.

Given the nature of this case, not only were the legitimate media there, but the Fleet Street tabloid journalists were jostling for position, eager to photograph and report this head-on confrontation between Judy and Martina. There were television cameras in the hallway, and CNN was prepared to broadcast the proceedings live from inside the courtroom.

Martina, her publicist (Linda Dozeretz), and Mike McCurly all talked to the press before entering the courthouse. They came out of the gate with a well-rehearsed script, introducing statements in the hallway that later would come out on the stand as testimony. Judy also met the press, but hers was more of an individual, outsider's effort to "set the record straight" and, hopefully, gain greater public sympathy and support for her position in these legal maneuverings.

Presiding over the hearing was retired Texas judge Harry Hopkins, who had chosen to come out of retirement, eager for one last hurrah. His rationale had been that his docket was clear and he could help expedite the legal process in a busy venue, but self-interest was clearly a much greater motivation. Harry's driving desire to try a famous "off-color" celebrity scandal case was obvious to all those who watched the events of the week unfold before them. The attorneys, filling in as actors onstage for the "Judge Hopkins Show," seemed too busy to fully appreciate the antics of this eccentric man. His legal procedures were sound, but his blatantly personal fawning interaction with the press was painfully embarrassing to everybody.

Judge Hopkins wasted no time trying to establish a cooperative relationship with the press. Prior to the hearing, when he arrived at his courtroom and saw about a dozen reporters from the British press, he invited them into his chamber. Once inside, he asked them to sign their names and send him "a little message" on notebook paper. He explained he wanted souvenirs from them, then requested that they write some kind of personalized message to him. Harry shared stories of American culture with the reporters and told them about his favorite Western television show, *Have Gun, Will Travel*. His business card had the slogan "Have Gavel, Will Travel." He gave all twelve members of the English press this card, obviously regarding himself as an independent maverick, a Western folk hero. But some reporters had questions about this bizarre episode and were shocked by his lack of professional distance. Obviously he felt this case was somehow different, that two women challenging and defending a same-sex partnership agreement of this nature—in Texas, by God!—was not to be taken that seriously. It was easier to go showbiz, to make a vaudeville show of the proceedings, than to accept the challenge that this hearing could set the stage for a landmark, precedent-setting civil-rights case. After all, large legal victories often grow out of rather small challenges by people who finally break either a social norm or challenge a legal point.

Jerry Loftin's first request of the judge was that reporters and cameramen should remain outside the courtroom. He was concerned that the legal atmosphere would be seriously disrupted and that this might interfere with the ability of witnesses to concentrate as they testified. Jerry was also concerned about protecting Judy's privacy as best he could.

Judge Hopkins had apparently advised counsel that he would ban cameras and microphones only if both parties requested it. So Loftin's position was foredoomed when Michael McCurly opened his comments in front of the cameras, grabbing this opportunity to charm and seduce the media. He stated that he saw nothing wrong with allowing the press access to the trial, making a pitch for public access and accountability as pillars of American democracy. McCurly further protested that Loftin was too late to introduce his motion, that the issue should have been anticipated and resolved earlier. Subsequently, Judge Hopkins refused Loftin's motion, and from that moment on, rather than trying to control the press, the judge encouraged their coverage and interacted with them on a regular basis. Harry Hopkins had come out of retirement to hear this case, and, by God, he was going to play it for all it was worth. So what could have been the perfect opportunity to challenge stereotypes about Texas justice instead turned into a display of Wild West shenanigans. While Judge Hopkins's actions might seem endearing and harmless, any judge is responsible for setting and controlling the courtroom environment. The all-important decorum of the courtroom was virtually ignored all week, from the moment the press arrived until the moment they left.

After granting the press admittance to the courtroom, Judge Hopkins invited them to sit in the unoccupied jury box, armed with long-lens cameras and boom mikes. He allowed other high-tech recording equipment to be placed throughout the courtroom, guaranteeing that in this hearing the participants would have few private moments. Even the conversations between attorney and client—whispers from twenty feet away—could be recorded and later played back through a sound amplifier at the studio. Each witness was fully aware that anything he or she said could be used in a broadcast. Needless to say, this kind of intrusion alters the legal process, and what should be a court of law becomes an arena for the commercial exploitation of celebrities. In all fairness, the judge asked if whispers could be picked up by the equipment. Mr. Orsinger, representing Loftin, addressed the court with his concern; "I have noticed that some of the cameras appear to have shotgun microphones on them. I don't know for a fact that this technology works; but if those mikes can pick up whispered discussions at counsel table, I am going to object that that would be an intrusion on the attorney/client privilege and work-product doctrine and I think we ought to ask these camera people to what extent their microphones are sensitive to these proceedings."

Hopkins then turned to the press and asked them, "Those of you that have microphones, let me see your hands. You have heard the matter raised by Mr. Orsinger in reference to your microphones and what they can pick up."

Several people piped up, "No we can barely hear what is being said."

Hopkins replied quickly, "Your viewers may be fortunate. All right. Does that satisfy you?"

Knowing that the judge had asked only half of the question, Loftin sarcastically replied, "Oh, yeah."

DAY ONE

Judy and Martina had not been in the same room together for several months, and both seemed visibly shaken when they first saw each other in the courtroom, each arriving with their legal staffs. Martina was also accompanied by her assistant Nancy Falconer, her friend Nancy Lieberman (the former professional basketball player and her former athletic trainer), and two other women who were rumored to be Martina's bodyguards.

Initially, Martina avoided Judy's glances, but Judy continued to look at Martina throughout the day. Martina must have felt her eyes upon her but avoided eye contact most of the day. Martina was scheduled to testify and—outwardly—she seemed well prepared for the challenge, but before stepping down from the stand, she would be overwhelmed with emotions and unable to hold back her tears.

There were important social and legal questions to be addressed that week in *Nelson* v. *Navratilova*, but they were undermined by the sensational and emotional elements of the case. Ideally, Judy and Martina would test the notion that two people could live their lives together, in a free nation, and then ask its system of justice—which barely recognized their same-sex existence—to protect their right to enter into a fairly straightforward contract that gave them the same financial responsibilities shared by the general population. Other cases before other courts had shared the same problems. In Georgia, at the same time, a case between two women who had entered into a similar contract was being decided. *Crooke* v. *Gilden*, minus the presence of a celebrity, was argued in a straightforward manner, and the state of Georgia upheld their right to enter into such a partnership agreement.

The Nelson/Navratilova case would be different, the proceedings muddied constantly by the presence and conflicts of power, money, and fame. Both parties felt passionate about their positions, but Martina and Judy had spent the last seven years living together in a loving, committed relationship. Each woman was now asking herself to turn on the other person she had most trusted and relied upon for comfort and support. And while they entered that Fort Worth courtroom armed with competent attorneys who had created sound legal strategies, neither woman appeared ready to do battle. They both seemed smaller than life and quite vulnerable to the process. It wasn't as though they were unprepared for the legal and media scrutiny they had to endure, but they had been separated only six months, and neither one appeared emotionally well armored or insulated.

Martina felt she was right and that she needed to see this case through, but she had not factored in the rigorous nature of the legal process nor the personal resolve of her opponent. Traditionally, business conflicts for Martina were resolved by her staff long before she had to become involved in the process. It was highly unusual for her to do any face-to-face battle anywhere other than on a tennis court. Yet now here she was in a courtroom, forced to talk about her relationship with Judy Nelson in front of live cameras and under oath.

Once the issue of press attendance inside the courtroom had been resolved, the hearing moved quickly. The hearing started out with a bang, as Martina took the stand as the first witness and presented her case at the opening, setting the stage for worldwide television coverage. Her strategy was evident. Her move to disqualify Jerry Loftin had several consequences with long-range implications, and now the battle had begun. Basically, McCurly would try to argue the eventual, anticipated *Nelson* v. *Navratilova* case inside this hearing. He planted the idea that this agreement was not a partnership agreement, but a palimony contract. This was not a bad strategy. While the contents of the contract were clearly partnership terms, the title is "A Nonmarital Cohabitation Agreement." So it would make sense for the defense (Martina responding to Judy's lawsuit), to argue the cohabitation angle for two reasons.

The first and best reason is that the state of Texas does not recognize the ability of same-sex partners to enter into such an agreement. Even if it were legal, palimony cases in Texas would have a rotten track record. Moreover, alimony is not granted in Texas, nor is it a community-property state. The second reason this strategy might work well for Martina was that a victory, successfully removing Jerry Loftin from the case, would enable her to go after Jerry Loftin and BeAnn Sisemore in a scathing and more productive manner. Martina stood to get Loftin's $1 million worth of malpractice insurance as well as matching funds from his assets, which would recoup some of the loss she might suffer in her case with Judy. Thus the battle against Loftin had become more important and viable than the one between Judy and Martina. This move to disqualify Loftin gave Martina a chance to weaken Judy's offense by putting Loftin in a defensive position—not to mention that if she won, she would recoup all of her legal expenses (which at this point had reached about $600,000) and part of any settlement money owed to Judy.

Beyond all the financial considerations were the emotional ones. It would seem that going directly after Jerry Loftin and BeAnn would certainly be easier, fighting it out with others, than to take on a former companion and her family. Martina would be in the enviable position of aggressive plaintiff rather than harried defendant. She would face Judy again, but this time she would be serving, rather than returning serves.

Martina was now on the stand. She broke down when the videotape of the signing of the agreement was played for her review. As it played and as Martina testified, BeAnn Sisemore stood in front of Martina. BeAnn believes that Martina cried because she was not able to face BeAnn and say that she thought BeAnn was an attorney.

Jerry Loftin played the videotape of the signing, stopping at critical points to ask questions about what was being viewed. In the tape, BeAnn says, "You have both waived that right, the right to be represented by an attorney."

Martina, on tape, replies, "We both waive that right."

At this point, Loftin stops the tape. BeAnn has placed herself directly in front of Martina and in back of Jerry and is beginning to cry. She thinks that Martina will not be able to avoid the truth if she is looking directly into her eyes.

Martina begins to break, her voice becomes shaky, and Jerry moves in for the kill. He asks, "Martina, do you remember, is it correct when Ms. Sisemore asked you that very question, 'No, we both waive the right, that right to an attorney.' Was that your statement that night?"

Martina replied simply, "That is what I said."

Loftin pressed on, "And at that point in time, when the agreement was—before signature, before you ever signed it, did you make the statement that you waived the right to an attorney?"

Martina replied slowly, "Yes, I made the statement."

Tension was building. Jerry chose his words carefully. Martina was looking down at her hands. Jerry continued his cross-examination, never asking a question he didn't know the answer to, leading her down a tight, narrow path. "And did you also, when Ms. Sisemore made the statement that Jerry is not your attorney and Martina is not—doesn't have an attorney, you said you understood that, too, didn't you?"

At this point Martina was in tears. "I thought I had an attorney."

Jerry ignored her answer and responded only to her prior statements by saying, "And you understood that? This [the videotape] is a window. This is exactly as things happened that night, isn't it, Ms. Navratilova?"

Cameras were clicking all over the courtroom, reporters were pushing against each other crowding in for close-ups of Martina as she became totally overwhelmed. In the background of this drama was a struggle by McCurly to get permission from the judge to Martina to leave after testifying that day. She had planned an African safari and wanted to leave Forth Worth as soon as possible. Earlier, all concerned had met in closed chambers to discuss this possibility. Loftin insisted that he might need to recall Martina later in the week and that she would have to stay around, just in case. Judy was particularly miffed when she heard about these negotiations because she and Martina had planned the holiday a year ago. Judy had made the arrangements, and now Martina wanted to be on her way as soon as possible.

The people in the courtroom were decidedly pro-Martina. In fact, Judy's mother turned at one point and told Judy's father, "Now I know how Martina's opponents must have felt at the matches. It's no fun being the underdog."

Eddie and Bales popped in and out of the courtroom all week, in between classes, even talking with Martina during breaks. The first time Bales entered the courtroom, his face lit up when he saw her. She came over, swung open the gate which was dividing the spectators from the participants, and gave him a big hug. "How are you doing, big guy?" she asked. Martina holds a soft place in her heart for Bales, who will probably be the closest she ever comes to having a son.

Bales was somewhat bemused by the spectators in the courtroom. He asked honestly, "What are all these people doing in here? Don't they have a life?"

Toward the end of the day, Judy passed Martina a note, asking to talk to her after the court was adjourned. Would she meet with her alone? Martina agreed with a simple nod of her head. The two went into the jury-deliberation room and, behind closed doors, tried to work out settlement terms. They had not seen each other in several months, and when Martina closed the door, Judy asked Martina if she could hold her. Martina nodded and the two women embraced for only a moment. "She seemed somehow smaller than I had remembered her," Judy recalls. "I had on high heels, so I was taller, but it wasn't the height. She just seemed much smaller. I wonder even now why that thought should have occurred to me or what significance it may have had. I only know that I'll never forget that feeling."

When Judy and Martina emerged forty-five minutes later,

they thought they had reached a settlement. They asked the court reporter to stay late, hoping to record the agreement. But Martina's attorney insisted that they "sleep on it" until the next day, then announce the agreement. Everyone returned home that night anticipating an agreement announcement in the morning. Photographs in the *Fort Worth Star Telegram* the next morning showed teams of delighted lawyers who believed settlement was just moments away.

It was dark before Judy left Jerry's office that evening; Eddie and Bales had stayed to lend support to their mother, and the whole family seemed to feel a sense of relief that there was now an offer on the table. Everyone seemed relieved, except for Judy. She protested, "I don't know what all of this will mean to Jerry. Richard Orsinger says I should pay attention to the bottom line, that it seems like a good settlement to him, and that I can't stop Martina from going after Jerry. She is determined to do that no matter what I do, but it just doesn't seem right. I'm the one who got him into it. Even if Martina and I settle, if she continues to go after Jerry, we'll all be in court for a couple of years."

Frances and Sarge seemed certain that things would work out to everyone's satisfaction in the morning. The television was on during dinner and electronic images of Martina breaking down on the stand flashed on the local station. Everyone was silent as Judy and Sandra glanced over and simply watched. The local station aired an interview with Judy and after it was finished, all went back to dinner. "It will all end tomorrow," Sarge said.

"We'll see," replied Judy.

Judy and Sandra drove two blocks to her sister's house after dinner. She immediately got on the phone and began returning phone calls. Sandra watched the Johnny Carson Show and CNN (she wanted to escape with Carson, but felt obligated to see what CNN had to say about the case). On Carson, that night, a stand-up comedian told a joke about Texas justice. It went something like this: *A man was found dead with eight gunshot wounds in his head and chest. The weapon used was identified as a hunting rifle. Murder was immediately ruled out. A Texas judge ruled that it was a suicide and according to the police report, the man not only survived the first six shots, self-inflicted to his chest—reloading his rifle between each shot—he was able to shoot himself two more times in the head, before bleeding to death when the eighth bullet pierced his temple. . .*

That was enough for one day. Sandra retired to her room and packed her bag with all but one suit and a pair of jeans and a jacket. She planned to go to the court in the morning and fly home in the evening.

She imagined Martina was making plans to make a late connection with her African safari group. Judy planned to stay until Saturday; she had promised to go to Bales's football game Friday night.

DAY TWO

Something had transpired during the time Judy and Sandra left the courthouse that evening and arrived the following morning but Judy couldn't disclose any details, as the process had been blanketed under a seal of confidentiality. However, she was obviously upset, and as she drove to the courthouse, she turned to Sandra and said, "I don't think I can live with the new terms. I'm not sure we can settle this out of court." Judging by her tone—slow and deliberate—Sandra could tell Judy knew the best opportunity to settle had just slipped out of reach. Apparently, when Martina's legal staff rewrote the settlement agreement, points of simple clarification had become new conditions.

Judy arrived at Loftin's office at 8:00 A.M. and they went on from there across the street to meet with Martina's team in the judge's chambers and discuss the settlement terms. Judy made it clear that she could not live with the new terms that had been added overnight, beyond what she and Martina had negotiated without the lawyers around. Judy felt as though she had to set Loftin up for a fall, placing them in a classic Catch-22. The terms that would allow her simply to wash her hands of the whole process would set a trap in which Loftin could not defend himself.

"I can't tell you what went on in there," Judy told Sandra when she came out, "but I can tell you that the deal is off. We are going to resume the hearing in ten minutes, and Martina has to stay in case Jerry needs to recall her. Eddie is going to have to take the stand, so please call him for me and see if he can come down. This is going to get worse."

Judy's father turned and said, "This has got to be the worst day of my life." Sarge has always been quick to understand the process—it's intuitive for him—and he knew that once the attorneys came between Judy and Martina at this juncture, an opportunity had slipped away, and the attorneys would be in charge from here on out. There would be no turning back. His family would be systematically called to testify and would be torn apart at the seams by the press. A system designed to be adversarial had gobbled this family up and held them in its belly. They had lost complete control of the process that morning, and he understood that the people inside the structure would not be able to protect one another from inevitably public and painful moments. Even the innocent could not escape the aggression of battle. His comment was made at noon and, as the day went on, it would turn out to be exactly as he had feared. Before the day was over, his son Sarge, his daughter Jan, and his grandsons Eddie and Bales would testify in open court discussing their relationship with the contract entered into by Judy and Martina.

While Martina's side seemed to be working from a well-crafted, well-organized script, Judy's counsel took a somewhat spontaneous approach. Nothing was rehearsed, and rather than set the agenda from the start, Judy and Loftin would respond to one.

The strain was visible in Loftin's performance. He and BeAnn had spent months preparing for this hearing, and their families were beginning to resent the time taken from their lives. Judy and BeAnn worked on every detail, leaving no stone unturned, while Jerry was forced to work with a small staff fighting mighty giants. McCurly's charts and graphs were elaborate, and McCurly was well organized with assistant after assistant handing him perfectly organized data, well marked for immediate access. Meanwhile, Jerry had lost so much weight in the process that his pants were loose, causing his shirttail to fall out when he rose to his feet. But McCurly's delivery was fast and direct as he darted quickly from one point to the next, making it impossible for Jerry and his staff of two to keep up.

DAY THREE

Eddie took the stand today. When he appeared in the courtroom, Sandra asked him if Loftin or BeAnn had given him any instructions as to the process. "No", he replied, "but I talked to Ma, and I'm ready to take the stand."

"Great," Sandra thought, rather sarcastically. "Ma has tied his tie and made sure he has on the right clothes, but what is he going to *say* up there?" But she was beginning to realize that the legal team had to be relying solely on spontaneous honesty because they had no time to choreograph an elaborate show designed to dazzle or confuse.

Jerry posed the question to Eddie; "What did Martina tell you about BeAnn Sisemore?"

Eddie replied, "Well, I have always been curious about the law. I am going to law school. So I knew BeAnn, from Mom, did something as far as the law was concerned. I didn't know what. Mom told me that she was a paralegal. I didn't know what that was, and so I asked Martina what a paralegal was; and she explained to me that it was a legal assistant and she worked for you. But I had not met you at the time."

Jerry continued, "So, in 1985, Martina told you that BeAnn Sisemore also was a paralegal working for me?"

Eddie replied, "Right. I asked her if she had had to go to law school or anything like that, and she said no."

"Did Martina tell you at that time that BeAnn Sisemore was a lawyer?", Jerry inquired.

"No."

"Did you discuss what BeAnn Sisemore did, what kind of a job she had?"

"Yes."

"Did Martina tell you that BeAnn had had any law school?"

At this point there is rustling at the table of Martina and McCurly, whispering among themselves and note passing. But the rest of us are all ears as Eddie answers.

"No."

"What did she tell you about that?"

"That she had not gone to law school, that she, in fact, hoped to go to law school one day."

"And that was 1985?"

"Yes, sir."

At the close of Loftin's examination, McCurly simply stated, "Pass the witness."

On its own, Eddie's testimony was a powerful argument that Martina knew BeAnn's status all along. However, a son testifying on his mother's behalf, no matter how cogent or clear, holds little weight with the judge. Still, this interchange between Loftin and Eddie might eventually prove powerful in front of a jury. And that was Loftin's strategy: to bring the argument forth—to sunshine it—as future artillery. This kind of byplay went on all week as both sides presented their arguments and basically tried to ready themselves for further battle.

The larger social and legal questions would be posed, but never clearly answered. This was supposed to be a hearing to remove Jerry Loftin from the case. With both sides eager to slide into the court records statements that would later help them when *Nelson* v. *Navratilova* was to be heard, the lines drawn between the causes became blurred. Points that were meant to illuminate arguments for and against Jerry's removal were reduced to clever statements made by Loftin and McCurly directed at the Judge and press, created for the sole purpose of planting in our conscious and unconscious minds, impressions of the integrity of their clients, messages that would help them get one foot up on the upcoming case. Both sides jumped to their feet many times, objecting to the other's tactics.

First, McCurly objected when Loftin asked Martina several questions about the actual agreement. "I object to his [Loftin's] inquiries about the agreement. Now, he is going into the Case in Chief. This is a limited motion, and I object to the relevancy."

Later in that same cross-examination, Loftin countervailed with the correct observation about McCurly when McCurly capitalized on an opportunity to turn an objection into an opportunity to pad the record. Loftin immediately pointed this out to the court. "That is absolutely jury argument. That is not an objection." Try as the court might, the cases were divided only in theory, they shared the same witnesses, the same facts and the same attorneys. The Case in Chief and the motion before the court dovetailed at every turn.

It was time to call BeAnn Sisemore to the stand. As Loftin's paralegal, she had been in and out of the courtroom each day— typing documents, finding information in the records, and compiling the documents he needed for the hearing.

By the time BeAnn took the stand, she was drawn and pale and visibly weak. Her hands shook, and she almost completely lost her voice. She felt completely responsible for placing Jerry in the position in which he now found himself. It became crystal clear that day that the only real betrayal BeAnn committed was to herself by being too generous to her friends. She went against her own gut feeling that told her she should have refused their request to assist them with this agreement—one final time.

The most enlightening moment of BeAnn's testimony was when she was asked why she had participated in this process with the women.

"Judy and Martina had been talking about how they were going to have an agreement, and they talked to me about it two or three times though we never talked about the terms that it would contain. And one day, they asked me if I would get them a form. I said no. I didn't want to—just go get yourselves a lawyer, get whoever you want. Go get a lawyer to do it. I don't want to get involved.

"I really like both of them, and I didn't want to be in the middle of it. And they asked me two or three other times, and I went over—finally. I said I will go to the law library and see if I can pick up a form for you to go by. I didn't intend to type it or do anything with it.

"I took that form. I got it from the library. I went to the librarian. I asked her if she knew if there was a form in any of these books. She took me over to the section. It was probably the third time I had been in the Tarrant County Law Library in my life, and I went to the librarian. She took me over to where there were books, and she pulled out the Family Practice Manual, which we had in our office. I said no, I need a nonmarital cohabitation agreement, and she went to a section. She pulled it out. She made copies for me, and she handed it to me."

BeAnn explained to the court what she did with the form. "That night I took it over to Judy and Martina's house. When I got ready to leave, they asked me to type the form. All I can remember is there was a round table in that little room where they watched TV—it's by the kitchen. And on the table was the envelope I had brought them with the form, and they asked me if I would type it for them—they said they didn't want anybody else to know about it. This is private. And why can't you, as a friend, type it? And I said why can't you, as a friend, go get a lawyer? I mean, I wanted them to get lawyers."

Sometimes, suggesting to people that they need legal advice sounds itself like legal advice. During BeAnn's introduction, she sounded as though she was "advising" them about their rights and concerns. Orsinger needed to reveal BeAnn's motive for videotaping the proceedings, to provide the court with an explanation for her shrewdness. Orsinger asked, "BeAnn, what was your motivation in explaining to Judy and Martina what you did on the videotape."

BeAnn replied, "To let them read the agreement on the tape to make sure they understood what they were signing. I was going to notarize it, so I wanted to make sure they understood what they were going to do."

Orsinger further demystified the situation by asking BeAnn, "Have you notarized other documents?"

She replied, "Yes, sir."

Orsinger continued, "Do you have any ideas or views about what kinds of responsibilities you have if you are notarizing a document that someone is executing?"

BeAnn answered, "Yes."

"Do you feel any responsibility as a notary to assure yourself that the person who is asking you to notarize this document, in fact, is executing it for purposes and considerations therein expressed?" Orsinger asked her.

"Yes, sir," was her reply.

"Were you doing that the evening on the videotape to Martina and Judy?"

"Yes."

The issue of foul motive had been addressed and answered. BeAnn was not acting as an attorney, she was exploring Martina's and Judy's "purposes and considerations" as outlined by the notary block. But did Martina think BeAnn was an attorney any time before, during, or after the event? Orsinger asked her, "Have you ever had any discussions with Martina Navratilova prior to the signing of the agreement reflected on the videotape about whether or not you were a lawyer?"

"Yes," BeAnn replied.

"Would you relate to the Court some of those discussions," Orsinger prodded.

BeAnn's testimony would back up statements made previously by Eddie, when he had been asked a similar question. "Martina kidded me a lot about why I should go to law school and why did I settle for less, and why didn't I do more."

Orsigner required one more point of clarification on this issue: "Did you ever hear Martina tell anyone else that you were an attorney in your presence?"

BeAnn simply replied, "No, sir."

BeAnn was not only their friend, but she felt obliged to do whatever she could for them. They had taken her to lavish parties in London, in German cities and in Aspen. They were an imposing presence, larger than life in moments, and BeAnn found herself walking step by step into a situation that would cause her boss, Jerry Loftin, to look as though he was not properly supervising his employees. She helped with the agreement away from the office and on her own time, but Judy and Martina were his clients.

The question immediately arose: Was BeAnn the fall guy, and had Jerry really known all about it? It was a clever idea, but

BeAnn couldn't pull it off. She had worked for him for seventeen years and was a loyal employee, but BeAnn didn't have the emotional makeup. She had a young son, and she didn't make a good victim. She had too much to lose. Nevertheless, Martina and her attorneys disputed these observations.

McCurly wasn't convinced. He wasn't satisfied with the answers given by BeAnn in response to Orsinger, and proceeded to grill her in redirect examination. He came on like gangbusters during his cross-examination. He had two goals in mind: first, he needed to connect Jerry Loftin to the document in some way. Either Jerry had designed it, or he told her where to get it and what to do with it. He needed to establish Jerry's involvement, somehow, through BeAnn. Second, he was concerned that Martina had said that she thought the agreement, in its final form, had become far more complicated than what she had originally envisioned. BeAnn held the answers to questions raised about the agreement's path that began with its inception in 1984, and concluded somewhere on the timetable—if she could.

BeAnn had told the court in earlier testimony that she had gone to the library and got the nonmarital cohabitation agreement out of a brown book. BeAnn's only witness, the librarian, had died several months after assisting BeAnn with the document.

McCurly asked BeAnn, "[But] you went to the library and retrieved a form book?"

BeAnn replied, "The librarian retrieved it for me."

"Sure. Okay. And you said it was a brown form book."

"Brown form book," BeAnn echoed.

"And that was the state bar book, Family Law Manual, that everybody who does divorce law is familiar with?" McCurly asked, setting her up for something not yet obvious, but clearly drawing her in for a reason.

"Right," BeAnn said.

Then McCurly launched into the argument that the book was actually blue, not brown, and it had been for several years. Clearly, BeAnn hadn't noticed. Most law books are either blue or brown, and the mistake should have meant nothing, but Mc-

Curly had something concrete with which to place the first crack in her story. Had the book actually been pink or light in color, it might have been noteworthy, but a different dark color seemed to do the trick for McCurly. It opened the door just enough for him to stick his foot in.

"Well, let me ask you this, first of all: Did you know, ma'am, that the brown form book of the Texas bar doesn't even have a nonmartial cohabitation agreement?" he asked.

"The brown one I saw did," she replied.

"I see. Why don't you go down to the law library at the first break and check, and I think you will find that it does not. Will you do that for us?" After asking the question, a 1982 edition of the law book appeared. After arguing back and forth, the book was admitted as evidence and marked Respondent's exhibit number 12. Orsinger and Loftin argued correctly that it had not been established that this was, in fact, the same book BeAnn used in 1984. However, Judge Hopkins wanted to hear McCurly out on this point, stating that he thought the origin of the document was crucial information—either connecting Jerry to its creation or BeAnn's independent judgment and actions in connection to Judy and Martina's agreement.

Starting to crack under the pressure, BeAnn gave him the answer he was looking for: "I guess it's legal."

"That is not their words verbatim, is it?"

"I may have corrected their wording. I don't know. I don't have the piece of paper [with Judy and Martina's notes on it]. We sat and talked about it. They made notes on it. I can't tell you everything without that piece of paper. Somebody has it."

Now that he had BeAnn totally flustered, he dropped the bomb. "Ms. Sisemore, the truth of the matter is that those are Jerry Loftin's words, isn't it?"

Quickly, without hesitation, BeAnn answered McCurly's assertion, "No sir. They are not. Jerry Loftin had nothing to do with this."

BeAnn was forced to read page after page of the formal document. Clearly, notes had been formalized to fit the language of the form, but that did not mean that Jerry had been involved. It did give credibility to Martina's argument that "The agreement was more complicated than what Judy and I had discussed."

The next step in McCurly's plan was to drive a wedge between Jerry and BeAnn. Now he was going to be friendly to BeAnn. "Okay. Do you feel like you are getting a bad rap in all of this, Ms. Sisemore? Are you being victimized by all of this?"

"I don't feel victimized. Sorry," BeAnn replied.

Like a snake moving through grass, McCurly approached his victim. "You are not really the one that did all of this, are you? As a matter of fact, there was a meeting in your office, in Jerry Loftin's office, where y'all discussed, the two of you, about whether or not to videotape the signed agreement before it was ever done, didn't you?"

"I had nothing to do with that videotape."

"You didn't have anything to do with it? Well, we know better than that. We saw you on it."

BeAnn replied, her voice beginning to break, "It wasn't my idea to do a videotape."

McCurly had put her in her place. She was worn out. He started waltzing with her. "I know it wasn't your idea. That's what I'm saying. That is not really your fault, is it?"

BeAnn began to weep. "I wish to God I had told Jerry Loftin, but I didn't. Nobody wishes I had more than me. I have lost two good friends. I have betrayed my boss, I guess. But I didn't realize—I tried to help somebody. Jerry Loftin never knew about this. I guess I messed up. Yeah. No. I don't feel like a victim. I feel like the bad guy."

Patronizing BeAnn, McCurly said, "Bless your heart. Ma'am, let me go over something now. You kept this from your boss so you could maintain privacy for your two friends?"

"No," BeAnn replied.

"You didn't tell him because they asked you not to, or kind of did when they said they wanted it private. Right?"

"They said, 'We want this private and we trust you, and we don't want anyone to know about it.' "

"And you inferred from that that you were to keep it from your boss. Is that what you are telling us?"

BeAnn answered, "I inferred I wasn't supposed to tell anybody. I shouldn't. A friend tells me something that's not any of my boss's business, nothing I do with my friends . . ."

McCurly stopped her in her tracks. She was about to establish the fact that she did this on her own time, and she didn't feel obligated to report her personal activities to her employer. Instead, McCurly reverted back to the privacy issue. As though secrecy was part of the conspiracy to entrap Martina without the help of counsel. "What exactly did they tell you about keeping this private?"

She answered the question again. "That it was a private agreement and they didn't want anybody else to know and that's why I didn't want——"

"Well," McCurly interrupted, "it was a private agreement and they didn't want anybody else to know. But some guy is videotaping it. What's his name?"

"Part of Judy's family, Sarge Hill Jr.," BeAnn replied. There, now—McCurly'd got Judy's brother in on the act. Next, McCurly brings out pictures taken that evening, and asks BeAnn to point out Judy's parents. "Well," he said, "it wasn't all that private now, was it?" He failed to leave it at that, and soon established that Jerry and Martina knew each other and that Jerry had represented Judy during her divorce proceedings, and had also helped Martina with a will and a traffic ticket.

"So this lawyer that's representing both of these people, you want to keep this from him to maintain their privacy while all the while y'all are taking pictures of other folks at the ceremony. Is that what we are to believe?" McCurly barked.

BeAnn restrained herself, and in a manner honestly plausible, she answered, "I didn't tell anybody."

McCurly failed to understand the loyalty of a Southern woman's friendship.

DAY FOUR

"Expert" witnesses were testifying today, and they get paid for baffling the jury, so we'll skip them altogether. They are simply hired guns doing their job and then collecting generous fees for their well-chosen words. However, while one of them was testifying, there was a flurry in the hall. Eddie whispered something in Sandra's ear and she went out to the hall where the press was gathering around the women's restroom door. One of the guards told her she could go through. As she opened the door she could see BeAnn stretched out on the floor—the paramedics were right behind her with a stretcher. She stepped out into the hall to give them some room and just then Martina swung the courtroom door open and headed for the restroom. The guard quickly directed her upstairs. "Good," Sandra thought. "The press always follows Martina; we can get BeAnn out quickly."

They didn't follow her this time. They stood with their cameras pointed toward the ladies' room. A few minutes later, Judy walked in. Now BeAnn, the paramedic, Roland (BeAnn's boyfriend), Judy and Sandra were all crowded in this small tiled room, along with a stretcher. BeAnn hadn't eaten in some time, and she was dehydrated and overworked.

"BeAnn, I am so sorry. We have to take care of ourselves—remember, you promised. When we decided to go through with this thing, we promised each other that we would take care of ourselves. You have to rest and you have to eat." Judy didn't know what else to say. At this point, she was nearly crippled with guilt for having asked BeAnn to help her with the agreement.

Frances came in next and she just stood there for a moment watching the tubes of liquid draining into BeAnn's arm. By now the color was coming back into BeAnn's face. "Oh, BeAnn, you've got to get some rest," she advised her. Then she scurried out to tell Sarge all about it. BeAnn decided she felt well enough to walk out. The paramedic warned her that they could not take responsibility unless she left on the stretcher.

The press was still out there. Judy came up with an altogether good idea. There was a hallway to the left and to the right. Everyone was on the fifth floor, so BeAnn had to get into the elevator, but there were two paths to them. "Okay, this is what we're going to do. BeAnn and Roland, go to the right, but first, let's put our briefcases on the stretcher and cover it with a blanket. We'll go out first and go to the elevator with the stretcher, and they will follow us."

Judy and Sandra swung open the door and headed toward the flashing cameras while reporters shouted questions. That worked for about ten seconds. BeAnn and Roland came out and were spotted before we got into the elevator. All four of us were now getting into the same car when Roland went after a cameraman. Judy and Sandra slipped into another elevator and headed for the ground floor. "Enough drama for you?" Judy asked.

Philip Finn in the *Daily Express* reported it this way:

> "Jilted Judy Nelson was caught in a wild melee last night outside the court hearing her $16 million palimony action against Martina Navratilova.
> Roland Arthur, boyfriend of star witness BeAnn Sisemore screamed and kicked at a TV cameraman.
> Armed Texas deputies leapt into the crush as tearful Judy, forty-five, and her new friend Sandra Faulkner tried to protect BeAnn."

(Well, it was dramatic enough, but not nearly as dramatic as it read. And somehow, the word "new friend" sounded far too dramatic to Sandra.)

Judge Harry Hopkins was still cozy with the reporters. On Wednesday he had even addressed them in the courtroom, before the day's proceedings. "I want to express my appreciation for the consideration and cooperation that the media has given the Court," he said. "You have been doing you job under less than ideal conditions, and I understand that; and I want to thank you for the cooperation that you have given this Court and to its litigants and all concerned. And to our contingent representing overseas media, you have been the model of decorum. You are welcome in any court over which this judge presides. We appreciate you."

With this, several reporters removed their lounging feet from the rail of the jury box, took their pencils out from behind their ears, and waited for the next opportunity to phone in the gossip of the day. Several legitimate reporters were still covering the hearing, but mostly it was up to the tabloid press to send words and pictures to the outside world.

Meanwhile, on the front page of the Dallas/Fort Worth paper

that morning was a photograph of Judge Hopkins in his courtroom—seated, his hands outstretched, and surrounded by British
reporters. Rather than appearing to be presiding over the proceedings, the judge was center stage and in the limelight. He
seemed delighted by the press and somewhat amused by their
process and presence. Sandra could not remember seeing a judge
posing like that, at his own request, with six tabloid reporters
from London.

By now, Thursday, the American press had largely lost interest in the hearing, but the British press was staying for the show.
Charles Bremmer of the *London Times* provided the most cogent
explanation for the American boredom with the process when he
wrote, in his September 12 column: "Americans often profess to
be amused at what they see as a British obsession with titillating
news, but the difference has little to do with squeamishness over
matters sexual in this case. The reason for the lack of interest is
simply that in a country which regards litigation as something
between sport and psychotherapy, so-called palimony suits—
even ones involving homosexuals—have become quite common-
place."

That being the case, the press was forced to focus on stories
about the people involved in the case, rather than the issues
before the court. These dramas served as smoke screens so that
the real issues would never surface. If they could keep the attention on money and greed, then the legal facts surrounding the
contract would remain blurry at best. Divert attention from
Martina and the contract and keep the press's appetite fed by
allegations against Judy and her family. Tim Miles reported in
The Sun on September 14: "Tennis Ace Martina Navratilova
yesterday branded ex-lesbian lover Judy Nelson a gold digger
who grabbed all she could." Martina is quoted as saying, "My
crime is stupidity, naïveté and not loving Judy anymore—for that
I have to pay. I truly believed Judy loved me. But I wonder, if I
hadn't been a famous tennis player, would she feel the same
about me?" Martina kept the attention on Judy's character.

The facts relevant to this hearing made little difference to the
media; the agreement was discussed inside and outside the court-

room. Each side managed to manipulate the debate in such a way that the issues of the real case would become entangled in the issues that were relevant to the hearing.

DAY FIVE

Judy had not yet taken the stand, although she had been prepared to do so everyday. There were discussions about not calling her as a witness at all. Frustrated and angry, she sat beside Jerry Loftin day after day, listening to Team Navratilova build a case against her and her family, but Loftin continued to advise her to just sit tight. She made only a few statements to the press. One night she told Sandra, "As I sit and listen to all that is being said in court, I feel as though I am watching a movie screen. I feel removed, as though I am just drifting. I guess I am just zoning out. How could Martina go after her friends like that? Jerry never did anything to her, and BeAnn was one of our best friends."

Finally, Loftin and Richard Orsinger decided to call Judy to the stand on this final day. Jerry himself had been on the stand for the better part of a day, along with Martina and BeAnn. Judy was ready and eager to take the stand, after spending five long days listening to everyone's version of reality. Unfortunately, she was seated only one hour and put through the normal procedure experienced by most women in "divorce cases." For example, did she work? How long? What will she do now? Did she plan to work?

At one point Judy described how she and Martina first came up with the idea that a nonmarital cohabitation agreement form was something that might work for them. "Martina and I were at the U.S. Open one year and we were watching TV. It was late at night and sometimes they have those little things on cable TV and they say you can do this, and you can do that and, you know, get it at your local store. It was suggested—I suppose it was some advertisement for legal things—that forms are available for various kinds of agreements, that you didn't have to have a, you know—spend huge legal fees to come up with agreements. So we asked BeAnn about that."

Martina hugged Frances and, looking down toward the ground, said goodbye to Judy. The she picked up her cellular phone to confirm her most recent travel plans. She was late for her safari trip. Sunner and Nancy were sent with Martina to help her catch up. Martina left the courtroom first. Outside in the hall, McCurly did most of the talking before entering the elevator and exiting the courthouse.

Judy put on fresh lipstick and then faced the familiar crowd gathered in the hallway. "Is is true that you want to write a book and that that is the stumbling block?" one reporter asked.

"No," Judy replied, "It is more complicated than that, but I really can't make comments regarding the terms. I can tell you that free speech is guaranteed to all people in this country, and I don't plan to let anyone take that right away from me."

In May, 1992, Martina went before the bar association in Dallas and successfully argued Jerry Loftin's conflict of interest. The bar recommended a suspension, which Jerry did not accept. His case will be tried in Tarrant County's 141st Judicial District Court, the honorable Harry Hopkins presiding.

Let's Settle

Despite having a house that was decorated beautifully with a Christmas tree and poinsettias and packages of all shapes and sizes, Christmas 1991 was less than merry for Judy Nelson. Friends and family had flown in from New York, California, and Texas, all arriving with cheerfully wrapped bundles to exchange with one another. This was the height of the season in Aspen, and everyone was delighted to be there; the slopes were covered with soft, white powder, the shops and restaurants busy with last-minute shoppers, and the town sparkled with tiny Christmas lights. This was the place to be—and the place to be seen.

Unfortunately, Judy was caught in the midst of all this conspicuous consumption and high overhead at a time when she was frightened that she might not survive financially much longer. The legal battle with Martina had depleted all of her resources while she continued to have financial responsibilities to her sons. Bales was in a private school at Country Day in Fort Worth, Eddie was at Texas Christian University, and their tuition wasn't waived just because their mother was in the middle of a lawsuit. Ed continued to pay his half of education expenses. She needed to continue buying them clothes and paying for their flights to Aspen, while traveling herself to Dallas several times a month to meet with her attorneys.

Beyond normal expenses, Judy was accustomed to a privileged lifestyle. Her horses were boarded, she took tennis lessons, and she was seeing therapist Annie Denver once a week. Judy tried to keep up a good front with her friends in Aspen, knowing how important it was to her case not to let her opponent see her sweat, but she admitted, "Martina and IMG know I am nearly broke: they know the obligations I have and the resources from which I can draw. They have me just where they want me."

This Christmas, gift giving was not as spontaneous and joyous as it had been in past years. There was no invitation from Don Johnson and Melanie Griffith as there had been in the past. Martina was in Aspen for the holidays, and the two were not going to be invited on the same guest list. They tried not to run into each other publicly at places like the Caribou Club or restaurants. Life had changed for Judy in Aspen—everything had scaled down—and this year she would have to settle for small private parties with family and friends.

Surprisingly, Christmas morning at the Starwood house, Martina phoned Judy to say that she missed the family more than she had anticipated and wanted to know whether she could drop by and leave Christmas gifts. Judy invited her to come over. An hour later, Yuletide carols were blasting through the house, and family members and friends were singing along with the CDs as they filled their plates in the kitchen and headed for their places at the dinner table. Suddenly the doorbell rang. Judy walked behind the large fireplace that separated the living room from the entry way, blocking the view of the glass french doors, behind which stood Martina. As she rounded the corner, she saw Martina, alone on the front porch, amidst piles of snow shoveled to either side of her. In her arms she held gifts for Judy's parents and the boys (though not for Judy).

"It was a bit disquieting and completely unexpected," remarked Chantal Westerman, a guest and close friend of the two and a houseguest for Christmas. Martina was a little taken aback by the guests Judy had gathered about her on this holiday. Besides her sons and parents, Judy had several other houseguests who were also friendly with Martina. Rather than merely stand there openmouthed, they continued to serve themselves dinner.

Judy graciously invited Martina to join them for dinner. She accepted the offer, and everyone sat down together. Obviously, there was an undercurrent of unexpected unease. For one thing, there was the presence of Martina's former trainer, Joe Breed-love and his girlfriend, Michael Iott (Martina and Judy's dentist), and Chantal, who was a reporter on *Good Morning America*, and close friend of the Hill family. Chantal had known Judy and the family when she lived in Dallas, before moving to Los Angeles for ABC. Martina and Judy often visited Chantal when they were in Los Angeles; they were members of the same social circle and had several close friends in common. In Aspen, Chantal was simply enjoying a vacation, but any reporter in Aspen at Christmas could be suspect, and her presence clearly threw Martina.

After the meal, Judy and Martina wandered over to the stairway where they sat and talked to each other for about thirty minutes. Everyone orbited around them as they visited, but avoided interference. Chantal said she felt torn between letting them simply be alone and wanting to talk with them to reduce the tension. "It was so sad for me to see two people who loved each other so much reach this point. It was truly painful to watch them as they sat on the step quietly talking, trying to work things out with each other. I felt tremendous compassion for them both."

While they sat on the steps, Judy said that she asked Martina if she was happy, and Martina replied, "I am happy with my tennis, but my life isn't that great right now." Judy said that Martina then asked, "How are you doing?"

Judy paused for just a moment before answering the question, and with conviction said, "Each day is a little better. I don't really know what tomorrow will bring, but I'm growing—my sessions with Annie Denver are helping me so much. It's a slow process, but I'm getting there."

Martina seemed to get caught up in the spirit of Christmas; she was back visiting her home in Aspen where she had spent the previous Christmas, and for a moment the legal problems were on hold. Visiting after dinner, she and Judy acted more genuine to each other than they had been all year, acknowledging how close they had been for many years. Martina even confessed that she missed the family at Christmas.

In months to come, Judy would question Martina's motives,

feeling as though Martina's visit was more manipulative than sincere—and wondering if perhaps Peter Johnson prodded her to appeal to Judy's emotions, softening her up a bit before settlement talks resumed. However, it had been nearly a year since Martina waked out of the Starwood house with her skis tossed over her shoulders, the relationship with Judy suddenly ended, and the first time since then they had all been in the house together. The house hadn't changed much—everyone still ate dinner off the same large round glass table—but Judy's circumstances had certainly changed, and she was not nearly so nostalgic. She had very little money on which to live and she was beginning to feel the strain more severely every day.

In fact, Martina was quick to take advantage of Judy's position and had informed her, a few days before Christmas, that she was no longer willing to pay the gas and electric bills she had carried during the negotiation process. Regardless of the reasons for having taken such action, Martina must have felt uncomfortable, like a person sticking a hose down a gopher hole, forcing him out of his tunnel and into the hands of his captor. She had to have known that refusing to pay for gas and electric in the winter in the Rocky Mountains—totaling over $1,000 per month at the Starwood house—was not a small gesture of power. The legal battle had gone on for a year and had now reached the point where a simple straw might break the camel's back.

Striving for a settlement had turned out to be the nightmare they had never dreamed possible, forcing them to fight publicly and perhaps destroying any hope of parting as friends. They had proven worthy opponents in a nasty media campaign, put in place and kept in place by a system that is laborious and cruel, where celebrities are private only when they are without conflict or controversy.

While Martina now seemed to have the economics on her side, the balance of power had actually shifted. By now, everyone knew that Richard "Racehorse" Haynes was Judy's new head counsel, replacing the embattled Jerry Loftin. Racehorse Haynes is a celebrity attorney in Texas, better known for his work defending criminals than his calendar of civil cases, but Judy's situation had caught his attention and he felt confident in that he could hit pay dirt with this settlement. As if that weren't enough, he had teamed up with Steve Sussman and company, while waiting in the wings, was Gloria Allred of Los Angeles, who intended to come aboard as a feminist attorney working on Judy's behalf. Without a doubt, this was a more powerful team than before and would certainly motivate Martina to try her hardest to settle out of court. Especially in light of the fact that she had fired Mike McCurly, after he had charged her $700,000 for his services. It was rumored that Martina refused to pay $200,000 of the charges—which included several hundred dollars he was charging her for "air conditioning" his building on weekends. This was the bill *before* going to trial—at this rate, the estimated cost of a jury trial was staggering.

With McCurly and Loftin both sidelined, the contest had changed. Both Judy and Martina knew that they had a small area in which to work if they could reach an agreement during the time it took to substitute these key players. Martina planned to be in Aspen for the first two weeks of January, and she and Judy were getting closer to agreement all the time.

Unfortunately, Judy's attorneys, Susman and Haynes, trying to avoid leaks to the press, asked Judy to wait until they could draw up a confidentiality agreement, blanketing all the subsequent settlement discussions that were scheduled to take place that week. Martina was willing to go along with the confidentiality request, as she was eager to settle. But the letter required by both sets of attorneys, binding both sides to negotiate freely with assurance that nothing said in the room during the negotiation process would ever become public, never arrived. Judy waited ten days for a fax that would allow the two to sit down and negotiate. Each day she thought the fax would arrive and that they would not only sit down, but settle. Sandra even flew into town for the event, thinking naïvely that the letter would arrive, and they could finally work things out.

As it turned out, Judy's attorneys were drafting a motion to sue International Management Group, charging them with (among other claims) conspiracy to tortuously interfere with the existing Navratilova contract and breach its fiduciary duty to Judy. Judy was aware of these legal actions, but thought she would be able to confer with Martina before the papers were filed. What eventually came over Judy's fax was a copy of the motion rather than the anticipated letter. Filing a case against IMG may have been a smart legal move by Susman and Haynes to empower Judy, but it torpedoed the negotiation process.

Martina was furious. She had conceded many points with the whole settlement process and wanted to avoid further attorney fees. The friendly atmosphere of Christmas day was fading, replaced by the echoes of despair and mounting anger. Sandra recalled coming into the Starwood house and hearing a message from Martina on the answering machine: "Judy, this is Martina. Have you heard from your lawyer? I think we should sit down and do this now. I hope it is worthwhile to you to wait for the letter." The tone was cold, and her frustration with both the process and with Judy was evident. The battle seemed endless for both of them.

No sooner had Susman and Haynes filed the papers against International Management Group than Martina was on the phone with Judy again. She was so angry that she could have blistered the phone line, and Judy was taken aback by her rage.

"How could you file this suit while trying to negotiate with me?" Martina wanted to know. "Do you know that you are accusing me of . . . fraud?! Do you know what that means?"

Earlier that day, before the papers had been filed in Fort Worth, Judy had faxed another offer to Martina. Unfortunately, Martina had left town earlier than expected, missing the most recent proposal. She asked Judy to just "give me the idea" over the phone, which she did, but clearly this was not the environment to discuss the settlement, and they got off the line after a futile twenty-minute conversation.

Visibly shaken, Judy finished brushing her hair, then turned and told Sandra, "For someone who was not able to level with me when we were together, she has no problem expressing herself now." Judy was distraught over Martina's comments but felt she had to trust her legal team to take care of her, sensing that Martina was now, more than ever, willing to settle.

Or at least it seemed that way, until Martina finally read Judy's settlement offer. She proceeded to fax Judy a note: "See you in court."

Judy faxed back: "I *will* see you in court."

Like two dogs baring their teeth and growling, they didn't want to fight, but they were willing and able to do so if necessary. Their attorneys warned each of them to back off and await well-planned—and one step removed—moves designed to champion each of their cases. The two foes didn't like hearing this, but still retreated from their engaged battle and left it up to "the pros."

Martina departed for Japan, where she lost in the finals for the second year in a row in that tournament. But she proceeded to Chicago, winning the Virginia Slims tournament in three sets against Jana Novotna to break the all-time singles titles record held by Chris Evert. Despite all the emotional turmoil in her life, Martina played focused tennis.

The one thing Judy had not factored in, when contemplating the length of her legal battle, was Martina's probable appeal if Judy won and the court forced Martina to honor the agreement. Even if Judy won hands down, Martina could still appeal the decision and retain the settlement money during the appeal process. Judy would thus have to live for another year or longer without additional assets. It was fortunate that Judy hadn't fully comprehended this scenario earlier because she had felt she had control over the negotiations, and would not be the first to blink. Now, from her own perspective, she suddenly realized, her settlement urgency. "My God," she said. "I had no idea that Martina gets to keep possession of the money even if I win, if she appealed. I thought I would be awarded the settlement, then it would be up to them to get it back. I can't afford this battle—they are absolutely right—I can't fight them. It doesn't matter what's on the table, I'm going to have to take it."

Martina was unaware of this revelation, which eventually allowed Judy's new legal team to pull her through the bluff of her life. Judy was holding nothing in her hand, but had to pretend she had drawn a royal flush. She played her cards close to her chest and never blinked.

At this point, in an effort to help Judy, Sandra decided to call their mutual friend, Rita Mae Brown, for assistance. "Look, Rita Mae, you're the only person I know who can talk to both of them. I know you stay in touch with Martina, can you try to get them to talk? April will be before you know it, and we just can't go to court."

Rita Mae said she was already involved in the dispute. She and Martina were talking on the phone during Chicago, and Rita Mae absorbed Martina's anger while attempting to lead both Martina and Judy to the table. She was in the process of compiling a book, but she promised she would go to the tournament and talk to Martina, if she met her deadline.

Martina came down with the flu after the Chicago matches, which forced her to drop out early in the Virginia Slims of Palm Springs. This freed her to fly to Aspen, where she and Judy would resume negotiations. It would take ten days for both sides to finally reach a satisfactory agreement, but not before last-minute snags again threatened to bring about a jury trial.

March 12, 1992, supposedly the day for celebrating settlement, Sandra arrived in Fort Worth, Texas, where Judy and her parents were planning to meet her as she walked off the plane. On the way out of the airport, the two were cornered by reporters asking them about the book they were supposedly going to write. The questions caught Sandra by surprise because she thought the book deal was contingent on a settlement, which was still privileged information, not yet public. In fact, the talks were quiet and Sandra's understanding was that that the media was waiting for the April 6 trial.

Had someone tipped the media off about the settlement? While the reporters said they had traveled out to the airport to ask about the book, Sandra could tell by their questions, and their urgency, that they knew something she didn't know. She was surprised when they asked who had won. Lacking any specific details, Sandra gave them a popular answer she thought would be the correct one, regardless of the terms finally reached by Judy and Martina: "The attorneys, I suppose."

After they finished interviewing Sandra, they held a separate interview with Judy. Sandra was busy carrying her bags to the car and paid no attention to the questions they asked her. Later that evening, it became clear that they were asking specific questions about the settlement, assuming it had been signed prior to the interview.

As it turned out, Judy had swung by the airport to pick Sandra up on her way to the attorney's office to sign the agreement. Sandra, too, thought the agreement had already been signed in Aspen, but this is how she was forced to work with Judy under the constraints of her negotiation with Martina. She had to guess at conditions, putting pieces together when she could fill in blanks or read Judy's emotions or moods and deduce information from her actions and plans—but never asking for any specific details. Although they talked every day, she couldn't share any aspect of what was happening with the negotiations, so she had to read between the lines. She knew the end was coming, however, because suddenly no one seemed interested in talking about jury-selection strategy, and she was told to continue quietly writing the first draft of the manuscript. Everything just stopped. That meant a settlement must have been reached—perhaps signed—but not yet announced.

When they reached Susman's law offices in Dallas, the family went into a conference room located next to the lobby, separated by a large glass wall. What was being said was inaudible, but Sandra could see the family shifting papers back and forth. A phone call came in, at about 4:45 P.M., and Judy spoke to someone for two minutes. She then came out to the lobby and informed everyone that they were holding her interview until after the agreement had been signed. "How do they know if it's not yet signed?" Sandra asked.

"Good question; I'm not sure," she replied.

Suddenly the deal was off. The pace in the conference room picked up; people started moving rapidly from office to office. Judy was taken out of the conference room and sent to an office, secluded from her parents.

The only other people who could know for certain that the

agreement was still unsigned were Martina and her attorneys. Good journalists would obviously have to check with Martina's side for comment, and when they did, Martina was upset. Again, Sandra deduced that they must have agreed to not talk to reporters until *after* the agreement was signed. This made it appear that Judy had jumped the gun by about an hour, thinking she would sign the papers before the news broke at 5:00 P.M.

Judy was mortified. A sure thing had disintegrated and Martina now had the upper hand. Through the glass, Sandra could see Judy curled up in a ball, on the floor next to the telephone. A half hour passed before Judy was able to get hold of herself.

When they finally left Susman's office at 9:00 P.M. that evening, Judy announced to her parents that she would need to go back the next day, and everyone in the car was painfully quiet. Just when they thought they might be celebrating, a dark cloud of serious doubt appeared. The deal had fallen apart in the few minutes it took for them to drive from the airport to Steve Sussman's office in Dallas. It had to have something to do with the interview, and that would explain why Judy's parents were so upset when Judy stopped to talk to a journalist with NBC. Sarge was agitated while we waited for Judy to answer the reporter's questions. Now he was upset about the delay. "I tell you, no deal is complete until the signatures are on the paper," he said. "Deals fall through at the last minute all the time. Until the ink is on the paper, the deal ain't over." He must have felt as though it was continuing on forever. He said, "I just want to get my family back together." In addition, feelings between Judy and her brother were strained. He had apparently sold information and pictures to the foreign press. In his defense, he said, "I never sold anything I didn't think was mine to sell."

The next morning was Friday, March 13, and Judy was leaving to go to her attorney's office again. There had already been a postponement. Martina, in Aspen, was skiing that morning and wasn't going to make it to the attorney's office until late afternoon, so Judy remained tense. Would this agreement be signed or not? Judy didn't know. However, it was with some optimism that Sarge, Frances, Eddie, and Sandra were to meet Judy at

Bales's baseball game that evening, then go out to celebrate afterward. Later, Sandra phoned Judy from the car on the way to the ball game, but she said, "I can't meet you yet. I am still here; keep in touch."

"Yeah, I will," Sandra promised. "Do you think you'll make it to the game?"

"I hope so; I know I promised Bales, and I really want to see him play."

The next time Sandra talked to Judy was in the middle of Bales's game—after he hit a home run. She was still at Susman's office.

Several hours passed and the family was at dinner with Eddie and Bales, but still no Judy. Sandra made yet another telephone call. Judy answered and said, "It is all over!" A press release had just gone out and she was on her way to the lake to meet the family.

[LINDA DOZORETZ COMMUNICATIONS]

FOR IMMEDIATE RELEASE

March 13, 1992

NAVRATILOVA AND NELSON ANNOUNCE
RESOLUTION OF DISPUTE

FORT WORTH, Texas——Martina Navratilova and Judy Nelson announced today that the dispute between them that has been the subject of litigation in the 141st Judicial District Court of Tarrant County has been mutually and satisfactorily resolved.

In an interview with NBC taped earlier today, Navratilova said, "I'm just thrilled that it's behind me," she said.

Judy Nelson told NBC yesterday, "I feel really relieved. I feel real happy."

Nelson added, "Things are better for both of us." She characterized her relationship with Navratilova as "good" and said, "We want to be friends."

When asked what she had learned from all of this, Navratilova responded, "To read an agreement before I sign it . . . I still will trust people . . . I'm not going to become bitter . . . and leery of everyone who is nice to me."

Nelson said she was always confident that, if she and Navratilova met "face to face," they would work this out.

Still ahead is the related malpractice case Navratilova filed against Forth Worth attorney Jerry Loftin, which could be tried later this year.

Both Navratilova and Nelson wish one another well and do not intend to further detail the terms of the settlement.

Supplemental Statement relating to
Navratilova/Nelson Resolution Dispute

In response to a report on KXAS-TV in Fort Worth tonight, lawyers for Martina Navratilova and Judy Nelson jointly announced that the statement that a house in Aspen is being transferred to Judy Nelson is correct, but the balance of the story relating to property transferred is inaccurate. The parties intend to follow the confidentiality terms of their agreement and not to discuss further details.

Judy was completely drained. For all its pain, the process had given her a satisfactory financial conclusion. There were no lingering doubts about what might have, or could have been in the future, if only she had . . .

They turned on the news after arriving at the lake house. CNN, as usual, broke the story first:

"The two had parted on a friendly basis." Over on the NBC station, the reporter confirmed, "Judy is writing a book and she is certain Martina will like it." Judy waited a few minutes and with a sigh said, "I feel a little sad, but free and in control of my own life."

Everyone was filled with powerful emotions, but no one knew how to express them in the moment. This was not a victory, it was a loss—an ending.

When the long-anticipated ending finally arrived, it was anticlimactic. For one thing, it was midnight before everyone arrived home, and 2:00 A.M. before Judy's parents went to sleep. Sandra had to catch a taxi to the airport for an early-morning flight. The taxi was due to arrive at 4:40 A.M. Judy was scheduled to leave at 6:00 A.M.

"Well," Judy said, "we'll each be worse off if we try to sleep. We have to stay awake." Judy was surprisingly chipper for someone who was visibly exhausted, her head bobbing to stay alert.

Each sat straight up in their chairs as they watched *The Love Connection* and *Nick at Nite*. Judy had a relieved look on her face, and it was clear that she was looking forward—she would never look back again.

Judy Speaks

On March 13, 1992, after the settlement agreement was signed, via faxed signatures from my attorney's office in Dallas to Martina's attorney's office in Aspen, I drove to the lake house in Fort Worth, alone. I knew that in some ways it was all over—my life with Martina. It was my last connecting thread with her. In another way it was just beginning—my life with my authentic self. I knew I had come a long way. I knew the journey would be different now, that the image had been made clearer because of the process. Because of this loss.

I drove home. In my solitude I was acutely aware that I needed to be alone, to take some quiet walks in the fresh air of the mountains. I was physically, mentally, and emotionally exhausted. I felt suspended between pain and joy. I knew there was perhaps one person who could understand my state of mind and would ask no questions.

The next morning I flew to Virginia to visit my friend of seven years, Rita Mae Brown. She understood my feelings better than anyone. She had been Martina's close friend for more than fourteen years. Rita Mae lives on a 420-acre farm, nestled in the middle of the Blue Ridge Mountains. I spent five days there, mostly riding horses, taking walks, and when I felt like it, engaging in long, uninterrupted conversations. Being with the horses I loved, being alone with the mountains and nature, and being with someone who knew me so well (for we had both been forced to experience a lot of the same feelings as a result of our relationships with Martina) was exactly what I needed. A certain healing process had begun and, with it, the hope that indeed there would be life after Martina. Perhaps I would even find in those mountains in Virginia, away from the high-profile life of Aspen, the peace I sought.

After my visit with Rita Mae, I returned to Aspen. On a practical level, there was a house in Starwood that needed to be sold. On an emotional level, there was still work to be done on *me*. I was determined that this time I would not come up short in that process. I was ready and willing to put in the time and effort that it would take to find my true self. There were also plans to be considered about my future, and there was a need of time to be spent with friends—the ones who had helped me get through this heartbreak, this disaster.

But there was still an aftermath. I had to return to Fort Worth one month later to testify on Jerry Loftin's behalf at his hearing before the Texas Bar Association. Martina had settled with me, but now she was about to confront me on still another battleground. She had filed suit against Jerry Loftin, alleging that his decision to represent me was a conflict of interest and therefore · unethical. She was requesting that her allegation be reviewed by the Texas bar. This was a clever legal maneuver. The lawsuit in general was an effort on Martina's part to win back the attorney's fees she had thus far accumulated, and also an attempt to recoup her losses to me. If it worked, she would be way ahead of the game.

In my memory, it was a gray, rainy day. It was Wednesday, May 13, 1992, exactly two months after Martina and I had signed our agreement. I had flown to Fort Worth the previous evening—quietly and unannounced. How nice. I met Jerry and BeAnn and Jerry's attorneys at Jerry's office at 8:00 A.M. I did not know what to expect, as this was not a formal courtroom hearing. It was, rather, an informal questioning before a panel of Texas attorneys who were selected to represent the entire Texas Bar Association in matters of legal ethics—a group that functions to regulate themselves.

Martina had written them a letter requesting this hearing, and for that reason we had all assembled, much as we had done back in August 1991. The major characters were all the same, but a year older and, hopefully, wiser. The main difference was the lack of fanfare. That pleased me. The atmosphere was solemn, at best. Jerry appeared tired and drawn. He was a mere shadow of the happy, wonderful, funny, and sensitive fellow that I had known since junior high school. BeAnn was there, of course. She was as lovely as ever, but there an emptiness about her—there was no one there behind that brave smile. She was thin. Too thin. Her eyes could not hide the sorrow and the fear. I've never known a braver and more honest and loyal soul than she.

Martina appeared amid a group of chattering attorneys. I could tell she was going to be at her charming best. Her hair was shorter and darker, and her pants and blouse were a bit wrinkled, which is always one of the problems of living out of a suitcase. She didn't speak. She didn't even look my way. Perhaps it was easier that way. Perhaps she was doing me a favor.

The hearings began behind closed doors. All that was said and heard that day was confidential. We each were invited into the room separately. I was the last to speak. It was 8:00 P.M. before we were dismissed. Martina had asked permission to leave early in order to fly to New York for a meeting or a dinner, I don't remember which. She left sometime in the middle of my questioning. She did not acknowledge my presence even then. I have not seen her since. She did, however, during a small recess late in the afternoon, just before I was to be questioned, ask me about a piece of outdoor furniture that I had that was hers. I told her that I would send it. I only remember being amazed that she should be concerned with something so trivial in the face of such grave circumstances, where people's lives might be scarred forever. However, there are two sides to every story, and perhaps she felt that I was the one who had started the battle and caused the wounds.

I had decided to spend some part of my summer learning how to play polo. I had a million business details to tend to, but I wanted to remember my hard-learned lessons; I wanted to devote myself to taking care of *me*. Learning to play polo was a gift

I was going to give myself. It would take care of a lot of time and energy, if I was going to be any good at all. I just knew I wanted to try. To play a *game* on *horses*—what could be more fun? I had signed up for a polo clinic with a pro named Rege Ludwig, from Palm Springs, who held clinics at the University of Virginia. It was the best thing I ever did for myself. I fell in love with the game. I am forever indebted to Rita Mae Brown, who suggested that I try it. I had always thought of polo as being a game for only the aristocratic and elite. I found it was not so. Instead, it was a game that could be afforded by almost anyone who loved horses and could buy or lease a good athletic horse, (preferably a thoroughbred), who was fast and (in my case) very forgiving. I ended up borrowing horses from friends for most of the summer, and only now that I know what kind of polo pony suits me, am I trying to find my very own horses. Realizing how enthusiastic I was about the sport, Rita Mae offered me a place to live and a horse to ride for the summer if I wished to stay in the area and play polo with some teams. I accepted gratefully.

I worked hard at establishing new goals for myself—both emotionally and financially. I had to work. I had two sons supported equally by myself and their father. They were both going to college in the fall. I became busy setting up my own investment company and writing my book with Sandra Faulkner. Emotionally I kept on track by taking care of my beloved horses and some new friends. I loved the farm. I even took more polo lessons with Rita Mae from a wonderful pro from Alabama named Robert Lyn Kee Chow. Polo is my therapy. It clears my mind because, for those precious moments while on that horse and swinging that mallet, I can't think of anything else—absolutely nothing—otherwise I might get killed, or kill someone else! Polo is my retreat, my haven.

As way leads on to way, business leads on to business, and I had to again turn my attention to financial problems at home in Aspen. While I had decided to stay in Virginia, at least for the summer, transacting business from there, I arranged for my good friend and realtor, Philippe Jacquot, to rent my home in Starwood while trying to sell it. It was a perfect arrangement. Philippe is a thirty-three-year-old Frenchman who over the past two years since my breakup had become one of my best friends. He also was my listing agent for the house. Philippe has a charismatic personality and is extremely charming. He is a handsome fellow, and reporters from tabloids took notice of the relationship. Immediately, *People* magazine entered the guessing game as to my sexual preference. It still amazes me that sexual preference should ever be an issue, much less a category. To be yourself, to be happy, and to love another human being—what can be better than that?

Philippe was as good as his looks, and sell the house he did. This relieved me of a huge financial burden. There were still huge attorney's fees to be paid, and back taxes, because I had to borrow money on which to live while trying to reach a settlement with Martina.

When Philippe called to say that the house had been sold, I called my parents, and they agreed to meet me in Aspen to help pack my remaining possessions. This would prove to be another in a series of emotional steps that at some point would put final closure on my relationship with Martina. Just when I thought I had climbed over the last hurdle, there was another one—growth and knowledge are both like that—just when you think you have said it all, heard it all, seen it all, experienced it all, you realize you haven't. There is always another step. Actually, I like knowing that.

The task of moving out of the Starwood house was at hand. Sandra Faulkner had flown in to go through photographs with me. Along with my parents, Philippe, and a few very good neighbors we managed to pack the boxes and move the remaining furniture and pictures, and load it all onto a rented U-Haul truck that was to be driven by my parents back to Fort Worth.

As we were packing, Sandra and I looked through pictures that had earlier been taken off the walls and stored in the basement. Months earlier, they had been divided into separate piles. Martina had taken her photographs in April, when she had taken her trophies. Still, there were hundreds of photographs left for me to pack. Sandra and I stayed up late at night and talked about the days on the circuit and I remarked how fast things had changed. As I picked up pictures, I would remember story after story. By now, I barely had to say: "This was Brisbane in '84 . . . and Prague in '90 . . . . and the U.S. Open in '86 . . . and Chris and Martina here on Aspen Mountain . . . and this was taken just three weeks before she left." The nostalgia was mixed with some bitterness at how it all unraveled. Still, each day, letters or phone calls came from Martina's attorneys, still trying to resolve loose ends in the division of the property. Martin and I had not parted as friends, as we had earlier hoped would be the case. In fact, we were now reduced to hassling over lawn furniture. There was little left in the house. The master bedroom upstairs was empty. The books in the office where Martina had burned the fax in the winter of 1991 were all boxed and ready for the movers. All the pictures were off the walls. There were no signs of our life together, only ghosts and memories of a house filled by a family who once lived enchanted lives together.

On the deck outside the master bedroom, I came across the gold plastic chairs that Martina and I sat on during the signing of the videotaped agreement.

"Do you want these?" I asked Sandra.

"No," she replied. "I never want to see them again," she laughed. But as we carried them through the backyard and out the gate, we both felt as if they were large icons of some kind.

We returned to the basement, and I picked up the framed beach towel from Brisbane that read, "Martina and Judy 11–17–84." I stopped and took it out of Sandra's hands. I planned to place it in the truck myself. "You know, I will always love her," I said. "I am surely not *in* love with her anymore, but I will always love her."

Once the truck was packed, and the back gate pulled down and locked, the contents safely stowed, Mother climbed in the passenger side of the truck and remarked, "This is great; it's so spacious." Daddy got behind the wheel and started the engine, then pulled out of the long driveway, breaking a few aspen tree branches on their way out.

The closing of the house would take place the next morning,

and I needed to be out of the house by 10:00 A.M. But first, a last night in Aspen with friends. Everyone gathered at a pool hall just down the valley and had dinner and a few drinks, but all were prepared to retire early.

At 6:00 A.M. Philippe started spraying the rooms with fragrances and opening the drapes in preparation for the walk through now scheduled for 11:00 A.M., just one hour before the closing on the house. He was muttering something like, "Cut me loose, I am out of here." That seemed to sum it up for all of us.

After breakfast in town at Poppycock's (my favorite breakfast spot), Philippe and I went to the title company to sign the papers on the sale of the house that Martina and I once shared. That afternoon, I had one last appointment with Annie Denver. Annie told me she was taking me off her books. I asked her not to do that because I would be back. I still had lots of work to do on myself, and I didn't like the finality of it all. But this was closure—a new beginning. And Rita Mae always told me that when one door closes, another always opens.

I should try to address those things in my character that are less than perfect. Those are the most painful issues—and the hardest things for me to see. At times my behavior can be both irritating and infuriating. That pretty picture of Southern charm can sometimes turn into a controlling, even overpowering woman. When things don't go the way I want them, I become resentful and I begin, in my ever-so-ladylike way (and sometimes *not*) to manipulate the person or the situation to get my way. The sad thing is that I am usually successful. I end up having things go my way. A bad characteristic is reinforced, and I continue the pattern.

I was never aware that being controlling was a problem until Annie Denver helped me realize it. Certainly people had said that of me but I denied it because that was never my intention. I believed that I was "taking over" because I could do the job better. To me that translated as "taking care of" not "controlling" the situation or the person. I was taught that nurturing was my job and that it was a good quality—it was what a good woman was *supposed* to do. I did it better than anyone I know.

One day in therapy Annie said something to me about controlling. At that precise moment a light switched on—it was perfectly clear. I understood *at last*, I would never forget. We were discussing the fact that Martina suggested that I had taken control of her life. I hadn't seen it.

Annie said, "Judy, you are a caretaker, which means you are *taking care of*. You then have more control over a situation than someone else. You are in essence 'in control,' therefore you *are* controlling." I got it. That made sense because I knew I was a *caretaker*. I always have been. Annie said that it is *not* a bad characteristic if I try to control my *own* space, not someone else's.

There are two ways that I can deal with this flaw. One is that someone can confront me at that precise moment. The second is that I can *realize when* I am doing this and back off, listen to the other person. And show more respect for their ideas or opinions. The reason that I have difficulty with this is that at an early age I was given too much power. I was chosen by my parents to help mediate some problems. In retrospect, I never should have been expected to have sufficient wisdom to deal with adult matters. But I accepted the role and my life within the family was changed forever. Since then I've used that power to get my way. It always worked—unless someone was strong enough to confront me.

Martina never did. She chose instead to walk out of my life, out of the life we built together. She left me having to fight the person I love most. But by leaving, she forced me to find my own identity. Through the battle of *Nelson* v. *Navratilova*, I began to do just that. The two of us were ultimately headed for a court confrontation—only the court this time was an unfamiliar one. Had we not succeeded in reaching an agreement, it would have been the match of our lives. A match where no one would win except the lawyers. But the material things that were at stake, while important, were not the central issue.

The central issue is whether a woman is responsible in a romantic, life-partner relationship. I think we know what those responsibilities are in a male-female relationship and, although those roles are changing, the laws of the land frown on "love 'em and leave 'em." What if the relationship is between two women? Are we so unimportant socially and legally that our bonds are irrelevant in this country? Is a woman important legally only if one is in a relationship with a man? And does this sense of being second-class citizens which many women can now articulate, affect and undermine our commitment to one another? If I am "second class" and my life partner is "second class," do I have to give my best? Do I owe her anything at all or she me?

Obviously, these are new questions for our society. So long as women couldn't lead independent lives, these questions could never be asked.

What this ordeal has taught me is that we are evolving. There are some heterosexuals who are violently against same-sex relationships. There are many more who are not violently opposed to female-female bonds but who still believe negative stereotypes, who believe that a love relationship between two women is not as valid as one between a man and a woman. Sadly, there are many lesbians and homosexuals who have internalized these negative messages. They, too, do not accept or support such relationships. As you might suspect, they were the worst critics of my decision to fight for my rights.

What I also learned was how many loving, accepting, and understanding people there are in this country. For every prejudiced person, there's someone with a warm heart. What a gift to find such wonderful people! As for *Nelson* v. *Navratilova*, who won the match? I lost Martina, but I gained myself. I hope I have helped other people examine the status of commitments between women. If I have done that then it was a victory for all of us. The old ways of hate and hiding have got to go.

I believe that even Martina now understands that standing up for a woman's right to love another woman is worth fighting for. She has enough money now that she can take risks. I am very proud of her being a plaintiff in the class-action suit filed by the American Civil Liberties Union in Colorado, where an amendment removing antidiscrimination legislation was passed recently in November 1992. She was quoted in a *New York Times* article as saying that she would not pay taxes to a state that did not recognize her as a human being. So perhaps the answer of who won in our love match is that we both did in very different ways, even though the two people involved rode off in separate directions.

I know that there is a lot of work left to do for the causes I believe in and a lot of work left to do on myself. But I am in a tranquil place—a place I could not have reached without Martina. For me, ours was a love match that will live in my heart forever.

Index